BLACK & DECKER ®

CUSTOMIZING
your home

39 Step-by-step Projects for Turning
Your New House into a Home

CREATIVE
PUBLISHING
international

CHANHASSEN, MINNESOTA

www.creativepub.com

Contents

Introduction 5

**Customizing with
    Universal Design** 6

Walls & Ceilings 11

Applying Decorative Paint
    Finishes 12
Applying Wallcovering 16
Installing Interior Trim 20
Installing Polymer Crown
    Molding 24
Applying Tongue-and-Groove
    Wainscoting 26
Installing Ceiling Tile 29
Tiling a Kitchen Backsplash . . .32

Lighting & Utilities 37

Installing Incandescent
    Light Fixtures 38
Installing Track Lighting 39
Installing Under-cabinet
    Lighting 40
Installing Crown Molding
    Lighting 42
Installing a Ceiling Fan-light . . .44
Building Custom Light Boxes . .46
Adding a New Receptacle 49
Networking Your Home 55
Installing a Water Filtration
    System 61
Installing a Gas Fireplace 63

© Copyright 2002
Creative Publishing international, Inc.
18705 Lake Drive East
Chanhassen, Minnesota 55317
1-800-328-3895
www.creativepub.com
All rights reserved

Printed by Quebecor World
10 9 8 7 6 5 4 3 2 1

President/CEO: Michael Eleftheriou
Vice President/Publisher: Linda Ball
Vice President/Retail Sales & Marketing: Kevin Haas

Executive Editor: Bryan Trandem
Creative Director: Tim Himsel
Managing Editor: Michelle Skudlarek
Editorial Director: Jerri Farris

Lead Editor: Dane Smith
Editor: Philip Schmidt
Copy Editor: Teresa Marrone
Technical Photo Editor: Paul Gorton

Assistant Art Director: Russ Kuepper
Mac Designer: Jon Simpson
Illustrators: Jan-Willem Bohr, Steve Karp
Project Manager: Tracy Stanley
Photo Researcher: Julie Caruso
Photographers: Tate Carlson, Chuck Nields, Andrea Rugg
Scene Shop Carpenter: Scott Ashfeld
Director, Production Services: Kim Gerber
Production Manager: Helga Thielen
Cover Photography contributed by: Pella Storm Doors

CUSTOMIZING YOUR HOME
Created by: The Editors of Creative Publishing international, Inc.,
in cooperation with Black & Decker. Black & Decker® is a trademark
of The Black & Decker Corporation and is used under license.

Storage & Shelving 70

Constructing Built-in Shelving . .72
Building Glide-out Shelves 74
Building Recessed Wall
  Shelves 76
Adding New Cabinets 80

Doors & Windows 89

Securing Doors & Windows 90
Installing a Keyless Entry
  Deadbolt 93
Installing a Garage Door
  Opener 95
Installing a Storm Door 98
Installing a Tubular Skylight . . .100
Framing for a New Door
  or Window 102
Installing a Patio Door 108
Installing a Window 111
Finishing a Door or
  Window Installation 114

Landscape & Outdoors 117

Installing Landscape
  Lighting 118
Installing a Floodlight 120
Planting Trees 122
Preparing Soil for New
  Lawns 124
Installing a Sod Lawn 126
Building a Platform Deck 128
Pouring a Concrete Walkway . .132
Installing Brick Pavers
  Over Concrete 137

Index 140

Library of Congress
Cataloging-in-Publication Data
Customizing your home : 39 step-by-step projects for turning your new
house into a home.
       p. cm. -- (Black & Decker)
     ISBN 1-58923-046-9 (soft cover)
     1. Dwellings--Remodeling--Amateurs' manuals. I. Series.
TH4816 .C87 2002
643'.7--dc21   2002019398

Other titles from Creative Publishing international include:
New Everyday Home Repairs, Home Plumbing Projects & Repairs, Basic Wiring & Electrical Repairs, Advanced Home Wiring, Landscape Design & Construction, Bathroom Remodeling, Built-In Projects for the Home, Refinishing & Finishing Wood, Home Masonry Repairs & Projects, Building Porches & Patios, Flooring Projects & Techniques, Advanced Home Plumbing, Remodeling Kitchens, Stonework & Masonry Projects, Carpentry: Remodeling, Carpentry: Tools•Walls•Shelves•Doors, Great Decks, Building Decks, Advanced Deck Building, Sheds, Gazebos & Outbuildings, Finishing Basements & Attics, The Complete Guide to Home Plumbing, The Complete Guide to Home Wiring, The Complete Guide to Building Decks, The Complete Guide to Painting & Decorating, The Complete Guide to Creative Landscapes, The Complete Guide to Home Masonry, The Complete Guide to Home Carpentry, The Complete Guide to Home Storage, The Complete Photo Guide to Home Repair, The Complete Photo Guide to Home Improvement.

Photo courtesy of Armstrong Ceilings

Introduction

Every homeowner moves in with their own dreams of what their house can become. That's the appeal of home ownership, after all—having a place that is truly your own. This book will help you transform your house into something that is uniquely yours. Whether your house is an 1890s Victorian, a 1920s Craftsman bungalow, a post-war ranch rambler, or a suburban split-level, we'll show you how to set it apart from the millions of other houses that share its general architectural style.

This is the perfect book if you're just moving into a new house—either newly constructed, or a previously built home that's just new to you. Newly constructed homes these days often come with only the barest of finishing touches, providing a virtual blank canvas for displaying your own personal style and interests. And with a previously owned home, there's often a strong need to add touches that put your personal stamp of ownership on the house. Finally, perhaps you've owned your home for many years, but are just in the mood for some easy but dramatic changes that will make it seem new again.

In other words, this book is for anyone who owns a home.

In *Walls & Ceilings*, easy-to-do projects show how to use paint, wall covering, trim, or tile to transform your home's walls and ceilings from mere backdrops into distinctive elements of a room's design.

Lighting & Utilities shows you ways to customize the various systems to improve the everyday convenience, safety, and appearance of your home. Several projects explore creative uses of lighting; other projects focus on electrical service, water filtration, fireplaces, and network wiring.

Storage & Shelving provides solutions to the common household issue of "Where do I put it?" Filled with unique and attractive built-in storage projects, this section will provide you with ideas and projects for making the most of the space in your home.

Doors & Windows is full of projects that focus on personalizing these bridges between your indoor and outdoor home. This section begins with easy-to-accomplish projects aimed at improving the function and safety of existing doors and windows. It also takes you step-by-step through the process of installing brand new doors, windows, and skylights.

The final section, *Landscape & Outdoors,* explores ways to customize the home outside the four walls of your house. From lighting to lawns, decks to walkways, the practical projects in this section can help to make your outdoor home space safer, more functional, and more attractive.

In addition, we also feature a section on using concepts of *Universal Design* to customize your home for changing physical needs. Beginning on page 6, you'll find tips and ideas for incorporating universal design into nearly any area of your home, helping you to create a lifetime home that is open and adaptable to the many changing phases of life.

Customizing with Universal Design

Universal design is intended for all people. While standard home and product designs are based on the "average" person—that is, the average adult male—not everyone fits into that category. Some people are short, some tall; some have difficulty walking, while others walk ably but find bending difficult. And physical abilities change constantly, as do family situations. By incorporating universal design into your plans, you can create spaces that work better for everyone who lives in or visits your home, regardless of their size, age, or ability.

Universal design is simply good design that improves everyday living. For example, wide doorways make passage easier for a person carrying a load of laundry, as well as for someone in a wheelchair. Closet rods placed high and low allow easier access for children or shorter adults, as well as doubling the available space for clothes storage. More a way of thinking than a set of rules, universal design can be applied to any area of your home, from room layouts to light fixtures to door hardware. Following are some tips and ideas to consider when you are customizing your home.

Walls & Ceilings

• When natural or artificial light cannot be increased, light-colored walls and ceilings brighten a room, washing out severe shadows and reducing glare.
• Wainscoting provides an excellent balance between good lighting and low maintenance, protecting the lower half of walls from nicks and bumps while allowing the top half to reflect the light of a room.
• Matte or satin finish paint helps to reduce glare.
• Colors and textures in paint and wall covering act as aids for someone with visual problems. For example, textured wall coverings can indicate the start of a new room to a visually impaired person or anyone maneuvering in the dark.
• Grab bars in tubs/showers and around toilets promote independence in the bathroom.
• Handrails on both sides make stairwells easier to climb and safer for everyone.
• Acoustic ceiling tile will dramatically improve sound absorbtion in rooms with few soft surfaces, such as carpeting or soft furniture.

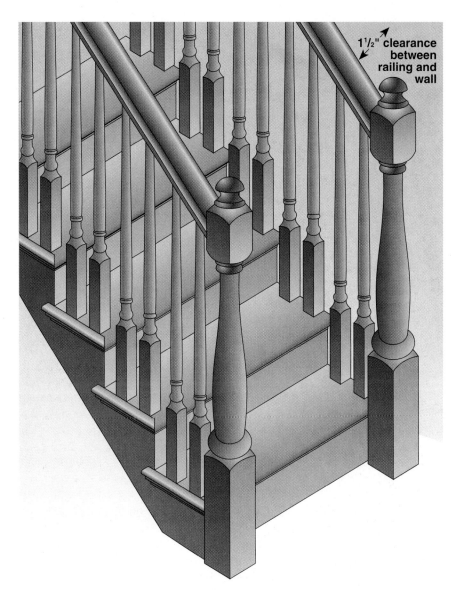

1½" clearance between railing and wall

Install handrails on both sides of all stairwells for balance when climbing or descending. Handrails should be easily graspable and mounted with 1½" clearance from the wall, allowing a person's hand to fit around the railing.

Lighting & Utilities

• Distribute overhead, wall, and task lighting evenly in order to create a safe environment, especially for people with vision limitations.

• Install receptacles in as many places as practical. This makes kitchens and other work areas more efficient, and increases versatility in living rooms.

• Install receptacles at a minimum height of 18", although 20" to 40" may be preferred. This makes it easy for both seated users and standing users who have trouble bending.

• Locate light switches at a height of 40" to 48", within the reach of children and seated users.

• Maintain consistent lighting throughout your home to aid those who have difficulty detecting stairs or changes in floor height.

• Look for fixtures that have at least two bulbs; this ensures there will be a light source even when one bulb burns out.

© Karen Melvin

Distribute lighting evenly throughout a room, giving special attention to task lights in work areas. The wide variety of fixtures available makes it easy to bring adequate light to a room without sacrificing style.

Rocker-style switches operate by simply pressing one side of the large rocker panel.

• Choose fixtures with bulbs that can be changed easily. Some ceiling fixtures have retractable cords that let you pull the fixture close for changing bulbs.

• Provide plenty of task lighting for activity and reading areas.

• Choose timed, motion- or voice-activated lights where appropriate. These eliminate the need to find and operate switches. (Make sure the fixture settings are easily adjustable.)

• Consider using rocker switches wherever possible. They are easy to turn on and off for those who have difficulty using their hands or someone with their arms full.

• Consider touch-controlled light fixtures, which don't require precise hand movements for operation.

• Consider using fluorescent bulbs where appropriate. They last longer and cost less than incandescents, and newer fluorescent bulbs come in colors that are pleasing to the eye.

• A bathroom is an especially good place for a phone, enabling a person to call for assistance, should he or she fall while home alone.

• Install switch coverplates in colors that contrast with the walls to make them easier to see in low light.

• Switches with internal lights help users locate the switch and may help someone orient in the dark.

Storage & Shelving

• Wall cabinets can be lowered to a height of 12" to 15" above the countertop to improve access without loss of counter storage space.

• Knee space under sinks or work areas accommodate those in a wheelchair or any seated user.

• Open storage bins provide easy access for often-used items.

• Pull-down shelving brings the items on the shelf to the user.

• Glide-out shelves in base cabinets make it easier to manuever large items in and out.

• Dual clothes rods in closets allow access for people of all heights and double the available hanging space.

• Many modular closet organizer systems provide easily lowered swing-down rods.

• Loop handles on cabinets allow easier opening than typical knob handles for people who have difficulty gripping.

• Shallow-depth, adjustable shelves offer better access and visibility in cabinets and pantries.

• Kitchen countertops with surface areas at various heights accommodate everyone in the home.

• Choose pantries with door shelving, as well as shallow, adjustable shelving inside.

• Consider color when choosing countertop and shelving features: a color-contrasted edge makes it easier for people with vision limitations to see the countertop boundaries.

Photo courtesy of Kraftmaid Cabinetry, Inc.

Pull-out cabinets like this pantry bring items to the user and eliminate excessive reaching.

• A clothing carousel in a closet brings your clothing to you at the touch of a button.

• Walk-in closets are a dream come true for clothing collectors, and a blessing for people with physical limitations.

• Look for low, shallow shelves that are easy to reach. Shelves should be no more than 18" deep.

• For wheelchair users, don't place drawers more than 30" from the floor.

• Wall-mounted shoe shelves paired with a nearby bench make putting on shoes easier for wheelchair users or those who have trouble bending.

• Lazy Susans in corner cabinets make for efficient kitchen storage.

• Vertical storage space with dividers spaced 3" to 4" apart can hold cookie sheets, broiler pans, cutting boards, or other flat objects without the need for stacking.

Photo courtesy of the National Closet Group

Closet organizers with clothing rods located high and low allow access to people of all heights, wheelchair users, and children. Low clothing rods should be installed between 20" and 44" from the floor.

Doors & Windows

• Lever-style door handles are easier to open than round knobs.
• Choose entry doors with low thresholds or no thresholds. The front edge of the threshold should be no more than ¼" high if it's square, ½" high if it's beveled.
• A good alternative to a hinged or sliding interior door is a pocket door. It saves space, requires no threshold, and can be equipped with hardware that is easy to use.
• Swinging doors are a good option in situations where locks or latches are unnecessary.
• A hinged sidelight makes a front entry door easier to navigate, especially when moving large objects.
• A keyless entry system is ideal for those who may have trouble operating traditional locks or anyone who hates fumbling for keys while standing in the cold.
• Provide a clear approach space, about 48" × 48", in front of each door.
• Frame doorless openings at a minimum of 32" wide (36" is preferred).
• Plan a clear approach space to each window, 30" deep by 48" wide.
• Position view windows at a maximum sill height of 30" to 36" so that children and seated people can see out. (Lower sills may pose a safety risk to children; be sure to choose your window heights accordingly.)
• Position windows so that hardware is at a maximum height of 48" if the window is operable.
• Tandem latches which operate multiple locks on a window with one motion simplify use considerably.

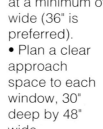

Lever-style handles open with no gripping or twisting required.

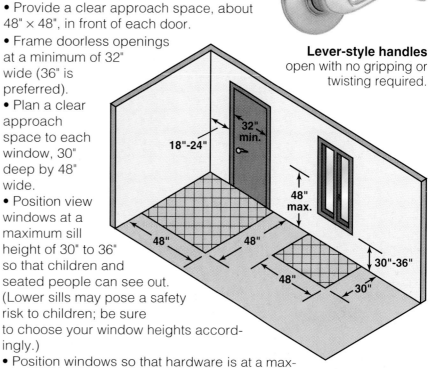

Raised planters allow people to enjoy gardening without the need for bending or kneeling.

Landscape & Outdoors

• Instead of traditional wooden entry ramps, build up gently sloped earthen berms to create unintrusive, accessible entrances which can actually add value to your home. By incorporating landscape elements such as paved paths, plants, bridges and retaining walls into the design, these earth ramps can be both a practical and attractive addition to your home.
• Install concrete walkways around your house to allow an even surface for those with difficulty walking or in wheelchairs.
• Texturize your concrete to highlight certain areas. Slight ridges can signal a transition from walkway to driveway, aiding the visually impaired and improving maneuverability in low-light conditions.
• Use low-voltage landscape lighting to illuminate darkened walkways.
• Install motion sensor or remote control floodlights for ease and safety.
• Consider the lifetime of trees when you plant. Where will the tree cast shade when it is mature?
• Use raised beds to bring the garden to the gardener. Beds up to 3 ft. tall allow the gardener to stand while working. A shorter raised bed with a built-in bench would allow the gardener to sit and allow wheelchair access.
• Various raised containers (from whiskey barrels to hanging baskets) can make plants accessible without excessive bending. Containers also allow you to customize your landscape design.
• Choose plants based on fragrance and texture as well as appearance. Plant them where they can be enjoyed by all.

Walls & Ceilings

Blended Finish

Applying Decorative Paint Finishes

New paint refreshes a room, but a decorative finish also makes a bold design statement. This project explains techniques and tips for three easy but attractive painting effects: blended finishes, color washing, and stencil printing.

With the right tools and a little practice, you can master any of these effects, then use your imagination to expand or adapt the techniques for your own custom finish. Don't be afraid to experiment and make mistakes. There is little you might do to your walls and ceilings that a coat of paint cannot cover and correct.

Color Wash Finish

Everything You Need:

Masking tape, drop cloths, stir sticks.

For Blended Finishes:
Divided paint tray, wool paint pad or two-tone roller, wool finishing tool, latex paints, paint glaze.

For Color Wash Finishes:
Paint roller, paint tray, low-luster latex enamel paint (for base coat), rubber gloves, pail, flat latex or acrylic paint, natural sea sponge or 3" or 4" natural bristle paintbrushes, latex paint conditioner (for brush glaze).

For Stenciled Designs:
Transparent Mylar sheets, fine-point permanent-ink marking pen, mat knife, ruler, level, stencil brushes, craft acrylic paints or oil-based stencil paints, clear finish or sealer (for finished wood surfaces).

Stenciled Design

Blended Finishes

One of the easiest ways to give a bland room a makeover is to combine two or more shades of paint for a blended finish. Using decorative painting tools, such as a wool pad or a two-tone roller, you can give your walls a patterned, faux-finish look.

When choosing paint shades, consider colors that will harmonize with the room's existing colors. Use a monochromatic paint strip from a paint retailer to find a strip that goes well with your overall color scheme, then select paint colors that are at least two shades apart on the paint strip. For a subtle design, choose shades that are closer together; for a more patterned

effect, select shades that are further apart. Combining a contasting color with two shades of the same color creates a bold, eye-catching pattern. Or, choose a single color and a neutral shade, such as ivory or white, to create a soft, muted design.

Using latex paint is recommended because it is water-based, and easily cleans up with just soap and water. It is also safer for the environment than oil-based paint. Water-based paints, however, do dry quickly, which can be a disadvantage for blended finishes. Purchase a paint glaze to mix with the paint to increase the length of time it can be manipulated.

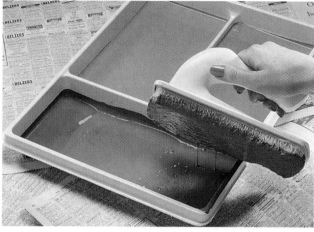

1 Pour each paint color into a separate section of the paint tray and mix ¼ cup of glaze with each color. Dip the wool pad into one color and scrape off any excess paint. Working in 4 × 4-ft. areas, apply the paint by pressing the pad to the wall in a random pattern, leaving some bare spots visible.

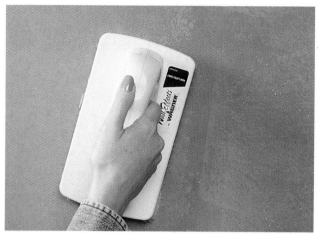

2 Scrape off excess paint from the pad and apply each of the remaining colors using the same stamping technique. You will begin to see the paint blend.

3 After completing a 4 × 4-ft. section, use the finishing tool to complete the design at the edges and corners. Dip the tool into one shade of paint and apply with a stamping motion. Repeat with the other paint colors, blending to match the finished design. Repeat steps 1-3 for the next 4 × 4-ft. section.

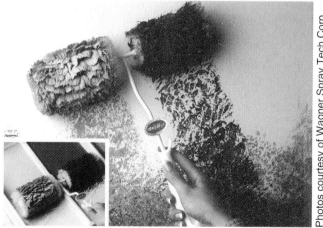

Variation: *Two-Tone Roller.* Pour each color into a section of the paint tray and add ¼ cup of glaze to each color (inset). If you want one color to dominate, add more of that color into the tray. Coat the roller covers and apply the paint using arching strokes that extend up and outward in alternating directions. Turn the roller over frequently to blend the two colors.

Color Wash Finishes

Color washing is an easy paint finish that gives walls a translucent, watercolor look. It can add visual texture to flat wallboard surfaces and can emphasize the textured surfaces of plastered or stucco walls. There are two methods of color washing, each with its own glaze mixture that creates a unique finished appearance.

The sponge method of color washing calls for a highly diluted glaze that is applied over a base coat of low-luster latex enamel, using a natural sea sponge. The result is a subtle texture with a soft blending of colors. The other method is color washing with a paintbrush, using a heavier glaze that holds more color than the sponge glaze. This finish retains the fine lines of the brush strokes to create a more dramatic play of tones. As the glaze begins to dry, it can be softened further by brushing the surface with a dry, natural-bristle paintbrush.

The color wash glaze can be either lighter or darker than the base coat. For best results, use two colors that are closely related, or consider using a neutral color, like beige or white, for either the base coat or the glaze. Because the glaze is messy to work with, cover the floor and furniture with drop cloths, and apply painter's tape along the ceiling and moldings.

1 For a sponge color wash glaze, mix 1 part latex or acrylic paint to 8 parts water. After base coat has dried, immerse the sponge into the color-washing solution. Squeeze out the excess liquid, but leave the sponge very wet.

2 Beginning in a low corner, wipe the color wash solution onto the wall in short, curving strokes. Overlap and change the direction of the strokes, quickly covering a 3 × 3-ft. section of wall.

3 Continue wetting the sponge and wiping on the glaze, moving upward and outward until the entire wall has been color washed. Allow the paint to dry. Apply a second coat, if additional color is desired.

Variation: *Brush Color Wash.* For the brush glaze, mix 1 part flat latex paint, 1 part latex paint conditioner, and 2 parts water. When the base coat has dried, start in a corner and apply glaze in a cross-hatching manner. The more you brush, the softer the appearance will be.

Stenciled Designs

Use stenciled motifs to highlight an area of a room or to simulate architechtural details such as chair rails. A variety of precut stencils is available in a wide range of prices, which usually are determined by the intricacy of the design. Or, you can make custom stencils by tracing designs onto transparent Mylar sheets as shown below. For stencils that coordinate with home furnishings, adapt a design from wallpaper, fabric, or artwork. Use a photocopy machine to enlarge or reduce patterns to the desired size.

When stenciling multicolored designs, apply the largest part of the design first. It is generally best to apply all the repeats of the first color before applying the second color.

Use high-quality, stiff stencil brushes in sizes proportionate to the space being stenciled. Use a separate brush for each color, or clean the brush and allow it to dry before reusing it.

For hard surfaces such as walls or woodwork, use craft acrylic paint or oil-based stencil paint in liquid or solid form. If the surface is finished wood, apply a clear finish or sealer to the entire surface after it is stenciled.

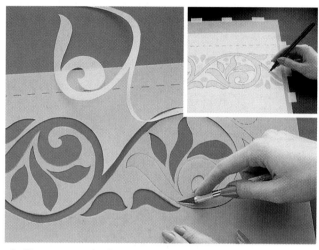

1 Draw your design on paper, repeating as necessary to create a pattern 13" to 18" long. Then trace each color area onto a separate Mylar sheet (inset). Cut out each traced area with a mat knife.

2 Mark a level placement line and secure the stencil sheet for the first color in place with masking tape. Holding the brush perpendicular to the surface, apply paint within all the cut areas of the stencil, using a circular motion. Allow paint to dry and remove stencil.

3 Secure the second sheet to the surface, matching the design. Apply the second paint color in all the cut areas. Repeat the process for any remaining stencils and colors until the design is completed.

Variation: *Stippling.* While the circular method shown results in a blended finish, *stippling* produces a deeper, textured appearance. To stipple, wrap masking tape around the bristles of a stenciling brush, ¼" from the end. Hold the brush perpendicular to the surface and apply paint using a dabbing motion.

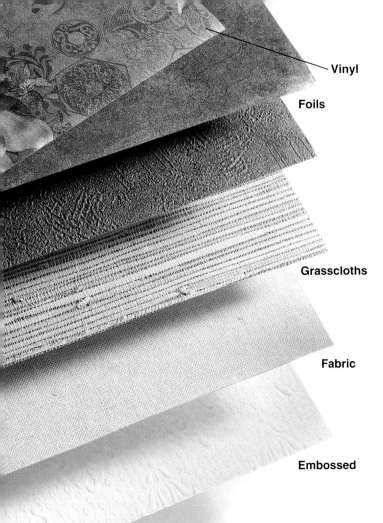

Vinyl

Foils

Grasscloths

Fabric

Embossed

Applying Wallcovering

Hanging wallcovering turns plain painted walls into elements of decorative design. It's one of the easiest ways to customize the look of a room. With the right tools and materials, and using the techniques shown here, two do-it-yourselfers can paper a room as well as a professional.

Today's wallcoverings may be made of vinyl, vinyl-coated paper or cloth, textiles, natural grasses, foil, or Mylar. Vinyl or coated-vinyl coverings are the easiest to hang, clean, and remove. Other types of wallcoverings can give a room a unique look but require special handling. Always follow manufacturer's instructions when working with specialty wallcoverings.

Everything You Need

Tools: Bubblestick, pencil, smoothing brush, scissors, razor knife, wallboard knife, seam roller, sponge, bucket, water tray (if using prepasted wallcovering), paste brush and tray (if using unpasted wallcovering).

Materials: Wallcovering, wallcovering adhesive (if not prepasted), vinyl-on-vinyl adhesive (if using vinyl wallcovering).

Tips for Planning Wallcovering Seams

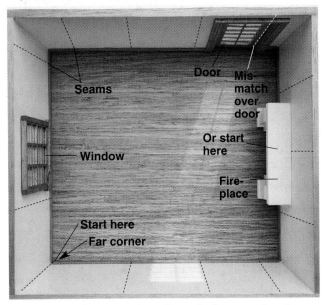

Seams · Door · Mismatch over door · Window · Or start here · Fireplace · Start here · Far corner

Sketch out the seam locations before you begin. Plan any mismatched seam, where a partial strip meets a full strip, for an inconspicuous area, such as behind a door. Adjust your starting point to avoid seams that fall in difficult locations, such as close to the edge of a window or fireplace. Also allow for a slight overlap onto the adjacent wall at corners.

How to Book Wallcovering Strips

For easier application, "book" wallcovering by gently folding both ends of the wet strip into the center, with the pasted side in. Let the strip cure for about 10 minutes. For ceiling strips or borders, use an "accordian" method by folding the strip back and forth with the pasted side in (inset). Some wallcoverings should not be booked; follow manufacturer's directions.

How to Apply Wallcovering to Walls

1 Measure from your starting point a distance equal to the wallpaper width minus ½" and mark a point. Draw a plumb line-from the ceiling to the floor at the marked point, using a bubblestick.

2 Cut the first strip to length with about 2" of excess at each end. Prepare the strip according to the manufacturer's directions. Unfold the top portion of the booked strip and position it against the line so that the strip overlaps onto the ceiling about 2".

3 Snip the top corner of the strip so the wallcovering wraps around the corner without wrinkling. Slide the strip into position with open palms then smooth with a smoothing brush.

 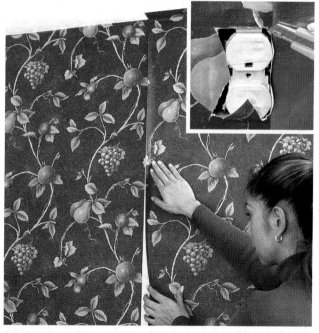

4 Unfold the bottom of the strip and use flat palms to position the strip against the plumb line (inset). Smooth the strip flat with a smoothing brush, carefully pressing out bubbles. Trim the excess wallcovering with a sharp razor knife. Rinse any adhesive from the surface using clear water and a sponge.

5 Hang additonal strips, butting the edges so that the pattern matches. Let the strips stand for about ½ hour, then use a seam roller to lightly roll the seam. (On embossed wallcoverings or fabrics, tap the seams gently with a smoothing brush.) With the power off, hang wallcoverings over receptacle and switch boxes, then use a razor knife to trim back the paper to the edges of the box (inset).

17

How to Apply Wallcovering Around Corners

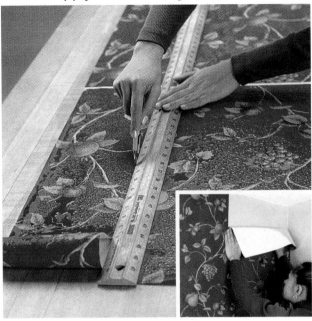

1 Measure from the edge of the previous strip to the corner at several points, then add ½" to the longest of these measurements. From the edge of a booked strip, mark the above distance at two points and cut the strip using a straightedge and razor knife. Position the strip on the wall, overlapping slightly onto the uncovered wall (inset). Cut slits at the top and bottom so the strip wraps smoothly. Flatten with a smoothing brush and trim the excess at the top and bottom.

2 Mark the width of the remaining strip plus ½" from the corner onto the uncovered wall and draw a plumb line from the ceiling to the floor. Measure the above distance from the leading edge of a new booked strip, and cut the strip with a straightedge and razor knife.

3 Position the new cut strip on the wall with the cut edge in the corner and the factory edge along the plumb line. Press the strip flat and trim any excess.

4 If you are using vinyl wallcovering, peel back the edge and apply vinyl-on-vinyl adhesive to the seam. Press flat and let stand for ½ hour, then roll the seams and rinse with a damp sponge.

Variation: Outside corners can usually be wrapped around without cutting the strip and drawing a new plumb line. If the corner is not plumb, follow the previous directions, but add 1" to the measurement in Steps 1 and 2.

How to Apply Wallcovering Around a Door or Window

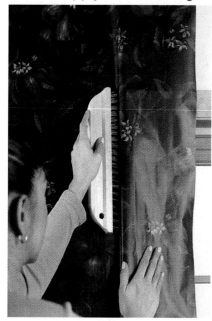  

1 Position the strip on the wall, running over the door or window casing. Butt the seam against the edge of the previous strip. Smooth the flat areas with a smoothing brush and press the strip tightly against the casing.

2 Use scissors to cut diagonally from the edge of the strip to the corners of the casing. Then trim away the excess wallcovering using a wallboard knife and razor knife.

3 Cut short strips for sections above and below the window. Hang these strips exactly vertical to ensure a pattern match for the next full strip. Repeat steps 1 and 2 for the strip along the other side of the casing, matching the edges. Rinse the wallcovering and casings using a damp sponge.

How to Apply Wallcovering to Ceilings

 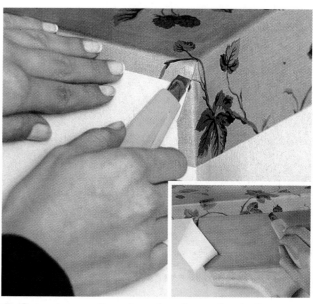

1 Measure from the wall a distance equal to the wallpaper width minus ½" and mark several points (inset). Use a straightedge to draw a guide line along the length of the ceiling. Cut and prepare the first strip as directed. Working in small sections, position the strip against the guide line. Overlap the side wall by ½" and the end wall by 2".

2 Cut out a small wedge of wallcovering in the corner so that the strip will lie flat. Press the wallcovering into the corner with a wallboard knife. Continue hanging strips, butting the edges so that the pattern matches. Trim the ceiling overlap to ½" on all walls that will be covered with matching wallcovering (inset).

Installing Interior Trim

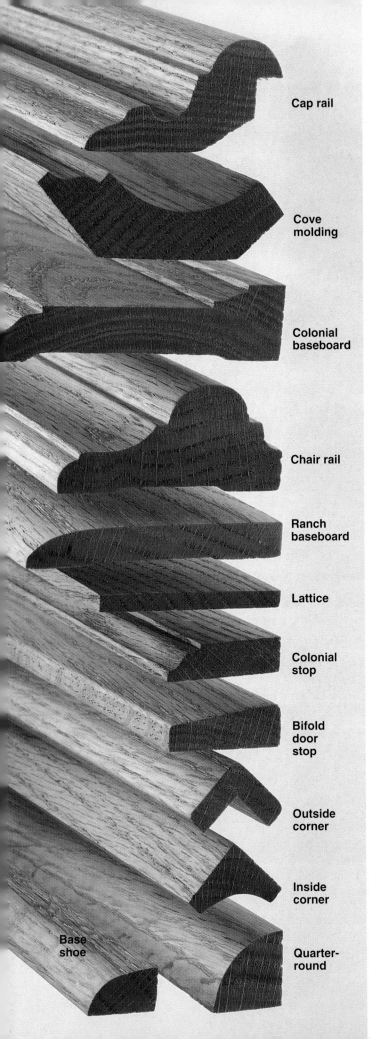

Cap rail

Cove molding

Colonial baseboard

Chair rail

Ranch baseboard

Lattice

Colonial stop

Bifold door stop

Outside corner

Inside corner

Base shoe

Quarter-round

New trim moldings can make rooms much more elegant and stylish, especially if you are replacing ordinary ranch-style baseboard and trim moldings with a more ornate milled style. To give a formal room a more dramatic look, there are elaborate crown moldings that form a highly decorative transition between walls and ceilings.

Trim is available in many different wood species, as well as synthetic (polymer) materials (see page 24). If you plan to install wood molding that will be painted, choose finger-jointed pine. It's less expensive than solid wood, and you can't tell the difference once it's painted. Choose a hardwood, such as oak, for trim that you plan to stain. Wood molding still offers the greatest variety of styles, but synthetics, which are lighter than wood and easier to install, are becoming increasingly popular for large or elaborate crown molding. Unlike wood, the polystyrene or polyurethane material won't rot, swell, or shrink, and it can be repaired with vinyl spackling compound.

Installing most trim involves the same basic cuts and fastening techniques regardless of the type, material, or style. Practice your cuts on scrap materials until you can construct joints that have no discernible gaps when you view them from a distance of 2 to 3 ft. When you're ready to cut pieces for the walls, remember that the corners of walls are seldom perfectly square. You may need to adjust the angle of the miter on some pieces and use caulk after installation to fill small gaps.

To avoid problems due to shrinkage after installation, stack wood trim in the room where it will be installed and allow it to acclimate for several days. Apply a coat of primer or sealer to all sides of each piece and let it dry thoroughly before you begin the project. You may also choose to paint or stain the trim before installing it.

Everything You Need:

Tools: Pencil, level, chalk line, power miter saw or miter box and back saw, coping saw, drill with bits, stud finder, utility knife, hammer or pneumatic nailer, nail set.

Materials: Trim, primer, 6d finish nails or pneumatic nailer nails, wood putty, paintable caulk.

Tips for Planning a Baseboard or Ceiling Trim Project

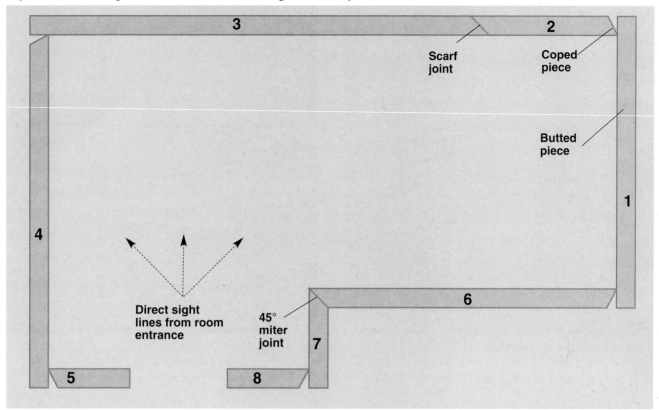

Plan the order of installation for your baseboard or ceiling moldings to avoid having to make more than one complex cut on any one piece. Use the longest pieces of molding for the most visible walls, saving the shorter ones for less conspicuous areas. When possible, place joints so they point away from the direct line of sight from the room's entrance.

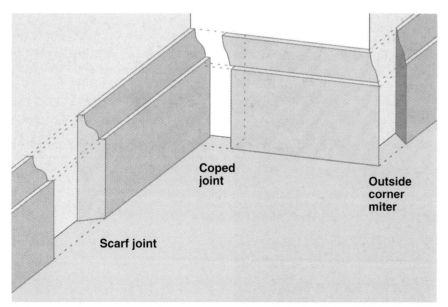

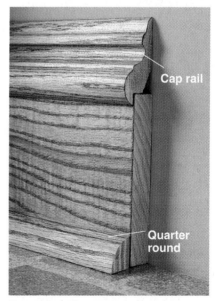

Join trim pieces using joints that are suited to their location in the room. For joints that run along the length of a wall, make *scarf joints* by mitering the joined ends at 45° angles. A *coped joint* joins contoured molding at inside corners. The first piece is butted into the corner; the second piece is cut and fitted against the face of the first. *Miter joints* are made from two 45°-angle cuts.

Dress up simple baseboard stock with cap moldings and base shoe or quarter round. Cap moldings are cut and installed at an angle, like crown moldings, using compound miter cuts (see pages 22-23).

Tips for Cutting Interior Trim

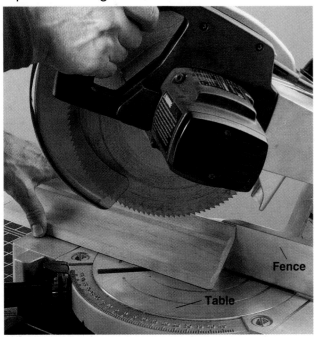

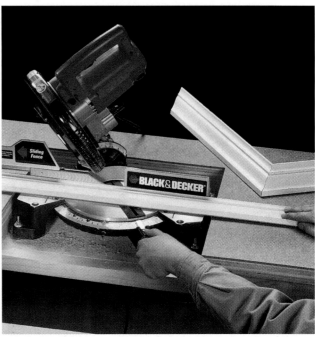

To miter-cut crown molding using a miter box or standard miter saw, flip the molding upside down, and place the flats on the back side of the molding against the table and fence of the saw (think of the table as the ceiling and the fence as the wall).

Variation: To cut crown molding using a compound miter saw, lay the molding flat on the saw table and set the miter and bevel angles. For outside corner miters, the standard settings are 33° (miter) and 31.62° (bevel). These settings on the gauges are often highlighted for easy identification.

How to Cut a Coped Joint

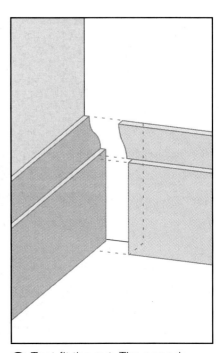

1 Coped joints form neat inside corners for contoured molding. To make a coped cut, cut the end of the molding at a 45° angle, so the back side is longer than the front side.

2 Using a coping saw, follow the contour of the molding's front edge. Angle the saw slightly toward the back side to create a sharp edge along the contour.

3 Test-fit the cut. The coped piece should fit snugly against the profile of the mating piece. If necessary, make small adjustments to the contoured edge, using sandpaper, a file, or a utility knife.

Tips for Installing Interior Trim

Mark stud locations throughout the project area, using a stud finder to locate the stud edges. Mark directly on the wall, using light pencil marks, or apply masking tape and mark onto the tape. Make sure the marks will be visible when the trim is in place.

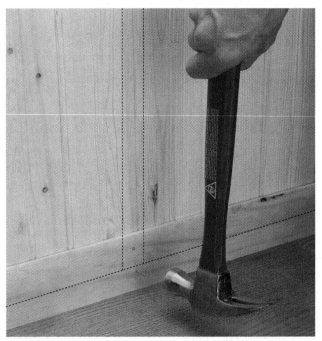

Baseboard molding is attached with two finish nails at each stud location: one into the stud, the other into the bottom plate. Drill pilot holes, and drive the nails at least ½" from the molding edges. Finish with a nail set. To prevent splitting, offset the nails slightly so they aren't in line vertically.

Flats

Crown molding should be positioned so the flats are flush against the wall and ceiling. Drill pilot holes, and drive nails through the flats of the molding at the stud and ceiling joist locations. Offset the nails slightly to prevent splitting.

Variation: A pneumatic nailer greatly simplifies nailing trim—it frees one hand to support the trim as you nail. A nailer also countersinks each nail automatically, eliminating the need to use a nail set.

Photo courtesy of The Balmer Studios Inc.

Installing Polymer Crown Molding

Add a dramatic accent to a room with polymer crown moldings. These synthetic moldings replicate historical styles and have the look of hand-carved wooden trims. Unlike traditional wood crown moldings which might include as many as seven pieces, polymer moldings are available in ornate single-piece designs that allow for easy installation. Special options include corner blocks, which eliminate difficult cuts at inside and outside corners, and bendable profiles, which allow you to mold around curved surfaces. The cost of simple polymer moldings is similar to that of pine, but ornate polymer moldings generally are less expensive than their multiple-piece wood counterparts.

Polymer moldings can be painted the same color as the walls or ceiling, painted with a contrasting color, decorated with a faux-finish design, or treated with a wood stain. Another option is to highlight the intricated raised designs by painting the raised patterns in one or more contrasting colors.

Everything You Need:

Tools: Hammer, power miter saw or miter box and fine-tooth saw, drill with countersink-piloting bit, cordless screwdriver, caulk gun, putty knife.

Materials: Crown molding, finish nails, 150-grit sandpaper, rag, mineral spirits, polymer adhesive, 2" wallboard screws, vinyl spackling compound, paintable latex caulk.

How to Install Polymer Crown Molding

1 Plan the layout of the molding pieces by measuring the walls of the room and making light pencil marks at the joint locations. For each piece that starts or ends at a corner, add 12" to 24" to compensate for the waste. Avoid pieces less than 36" long, if possible, because short pieces are more difficult to fit.

2 Hold a section of molding against the wall and ceiling in the finished position. Make light pencil marks on the wall every 12" along the bottom edge of the molding. Remove the molding, and tack a finish nail at each pencil mark. The nails will hold the molding in place while the adhesive dries. If the wall surface is plaster, drill pilot holes for the nails.

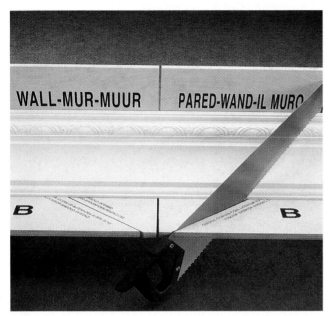

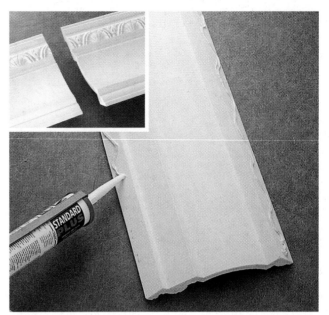

3 To make the miter cuts for the first corner, position the molding face up in a miter box. Set the ceiling-side flat of the molding against the horizontal table of the miter box, and set the wall-side flat against the vertical back fence (see page 22). Make the cut at 45°.

4 Check the uncut ends of each molding piece before installing it to make sure mating pieces will butt together squarely (inset). Use a miter saw to cut all square ends at 90° to ensure a tight joint. Lightly sand the backs of the molding that will make contact with the wall and ceiling. Wipe away the sanding dust using a rag slightly dampened with mineral spirits. Run a small bead of polymer adhesive (recommended or supplied by the manufacturer) along both sanded edges.

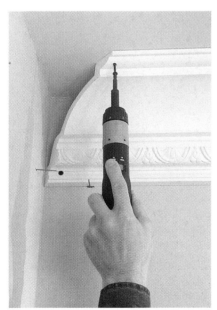

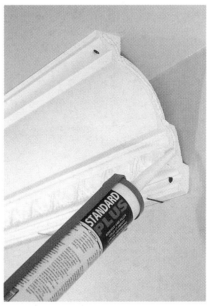

5 Set the molding in place with the mitered end tight to the corner and the bottom edge resting on the finish nails. Press along the wall and ceiling edges to create a good bond. At each end of the section, drill a countersunk pilot hole through the flats and into the ceiling and wall. Drive 2" wallboard screws through the pilot holes.

6 Cut, sand, and glue the next section of molding. Apply a bead of adhesive to the end where the installed molding will meet the new section. Install the new section, and secure the ends with screws, making sure the joints are aligned properly. Install the remaining molding sections, and allow the adhesive to dry.

7 Carefully remove the finish nails and fill the nail holes with vinyl spackling compound. Fill the screw holes in the molding and any gaps in the joints with paintable latex caulk or filler, and wipe away excess caulk with a damp cloth or a wet finger. Smooth the caulk over the holes so it is flush with the surface.

Applying Tongue-and-Groove Wainscoting

Wainscoting—a decorative wood finish applied to the lower part of walls—gives a room a distinctive, fashionable look. Wainscoting is installed for decorative purposes, but it is also useful as a protective surface for walls in well-used areas, like kitchens, hallways, and mudrooms. Depending on the type of finish and trim moldings used, you can create many different styles—from English estate to cabin quaint. Our example uses pine planking and a light finish to create a classic American beadboard look.

Wood wainscoting is available in a number of species and styles. The boards are typically made of pine, fir, or other softwoods, and measure ¼" to ¾" thick. Each board has a tongue on one edge, a groove on the other, and usually a decorative bevel or bead in the middle. Although typically about waist-high, there is no standard wainscot height, so you can choose what looks best for your application.

To plan your layout, first measure the reveal of the boards. Fit two pieces together and measure the exposed surface. Calculate the number of boards required for each wall by dividing the length of the wall by the reveal, keeping in mind that a side edge may have to be removed from one or more of the corner boards. If the total number of boards includes a fraction of less than half a board, plan to trim the first board, and last, if necessary, to avoid ending with a board cut to less than half its original width.

Before installing, condition the boards by stacking them in the room where they will be installed. Allow the wood to adjust to the room's temperature and humidity. Wait 72 hours before staining or sealing the boards.

There are two basic methods for installing wainscoting. Thinner material can be glued to finished wallboard, using construction adhesive, and tacked in place with nails. Thicker wainscoting material should always be fastened with nails. However, in order to use nails, you need to install backing. If the wall is already finished with wallboard, cut out horizontal strips of wallboard to create channels, then screw strips of ½" plywood backing directly to the studs.

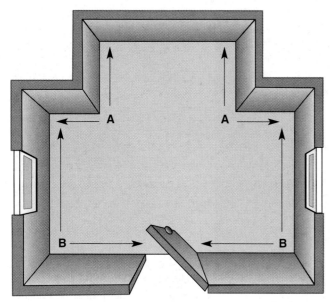

Begin your installation at the corners. Install any outside corners (A) first, and work your way in toward the inside corners. At outside corners, you can miter the boards for a finished joint or butt them together and cover the joint with corner molding. In sections of the room that have no outside corners, start at the inside corners (B), and work your way toward the door and window casings.

Everything You Need

Tools: 4-ft. level, circular saw, drill, nail set, compass, power miter saw or hand miter box.

Materials: Tongue-and-groove boards, 6d finish nails, baseboard and cap rail molding, wood-finishing materials.

How to Install Wainscoting (Starting at an Outside Corner)

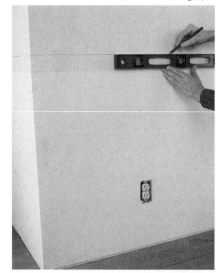

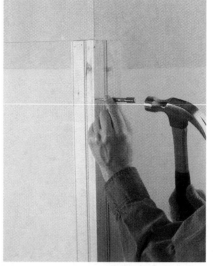

1 Turn off the electricity in the project area, then remove the-baseboard trim and receptacle coverplates. Mark a level control line along the walls to designate the height of the tongue-and-groove boards. Leave room for a ¼" gap between the boards and the floor for expansion.

2 Cut a pair of boards to width, based on your layout. NOTE: If the corner is not plumb, you may have to taper one or both boards so that the uncut edges will be plumb. Face-nail the boards in place, then nail along the joint, using 6d finish nails. Drill pilot holes, if necessary, to prevent splitting the wood. Set the nails with a nail set.

3 If the corner boards are butted together rather than mitered, nail a piece of corner trim over the corner, using 6d finish nails. Install the remaining boards along both walls (steps 5 and 6, page 28).

How to Install Wainscoting (Starting at an Inside Corner)

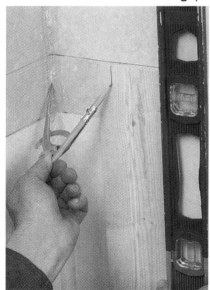

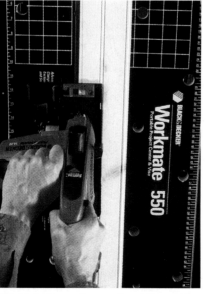

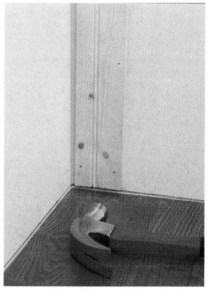

1 Check the corner for plumb. If it's not plumb, scribe and trim the first board to compensate. Hold the board plumb, then use a compass to transfer the contours of the wall to the board. Keep in mind the overall width of the board, based on your layout.

2 Cut along the scribed line with a circular saw. If you found that the corner was plumb in step 1, trim the first board to width, following your layout. If you're starting with the tongue edge in the corner, trim off at least the tongue from the first board.

3 Position the board in the corner, leaving a ⅛" gap for expansion. Make sure the board is plumb, then face-nail it in place with 6d finish nails. Drill pilot holes, if necessary, to prevent splitting. Drive the bottom and top nails where they'll be hidden by the trim moldings.

(continued next page)

How to Install Wainscoting (Starting at an Inside Corner) (continued)

4 Trim (if necessary) and install a second board at the corner. Butt the board against the first one and make sure it's plumb; face-nail this second board in place.

5 Install subsequent boards along the wall by gluing or nailing. Leave a ¹⁄₁₆" gap at each joint to allow for expansion. Use a level to check every third board for plumb. If it's out of plumb, adjust the next few boards to compensate.

6 Mark and cut the final board to fit. If you're at a door casing, cut the board to fit flush with the casing (trim off at least the tongue). If you're at an inside corner, make sure it's plumb. If not, scribe and trim the board to fit. Set all nails with a nail set.

How to Finish a Wainscoting Project

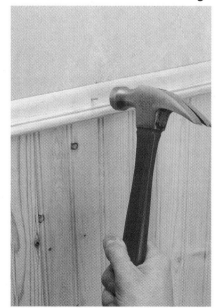

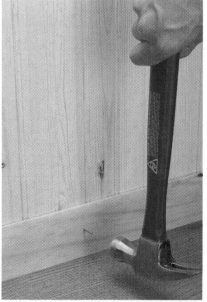

1 Cut and fit the cap rail molding over the top edges of the boards (see pages 20-23), and fasten it with 6d finish nails driven into the wall studs or backing. Set the nails with a nail set.

2 Cut baseboard molding to fit over the wainscoting, and attach it with 6d finish nails at all wall stud locations. If you plan to install base shoe, fasten the shoe to the floor, not the baseboard.

Tip: On windows with picture frame casing, install wainscoting up to the casing on the sides and below the window, then hide the joints with cove or another type of molding.

Installing Ceiling Tile

When customizing the look of a room, don't forget the possiblities above your head. Easy-to-install ceiling tile can lend instant character to a plain ceiling or help turn an unfinished basement or attic into a beautiful living space. Made of pressed mineral and fiberboard, ceiling tiles are available in a variety of styles and provide dramatic noise reduction as well.

Unlike a typical suspended panel ceiling, tongue-and-groove ceiling tiles provide an attractive, finished look with only a few inches of lost head space. Ceiling tiles can generally be attached directly to a wallboard or plaster ceiling with adhesive. If your ceiling is damaged or uneven, or if you have an unfinished joist ceiling, install wood furring strips as a base for the tiles, as shown in this project. Specially designed metal tracks are also available that allow you to easily clip the tiles into place.

Unless your ceiling's length and width measure in even feet, you will not be able to install the 12" tiles without some cutting. To prevent an unattractive installation with small, irregular tiles along two sides, plan a course of border tiles around the perimeter of your entire installation. Opposite ends of a room should have tiles cut to the same width. Follow the guidelines in this project to ensure that the border tiles are at least ½ the width of a full tile, allowing for easier application and a more attractive appearance.

Ceiling tile can be painted to match any decor. For best results, apply two coats of paint using a roller with a ¼" nap. Wait 24 hours between coats.

Photo courtesy of Armstrong Ceilings

Everything You Need

Tools: 4-ft. level, stepladder, tape measure, chalk line, utility knife, straightedge, pencil, hammer or drill, handsaw, stapler.

Materials: 1 × 2 furring strips, 8d nails or 2" screws, string, ceiling tiles, staples, trim molding.

Create an area rug effect by covering only a portion of the ceiling with tiles. This technique helps to define living areas in open floor plans by breaking up bland expanses of white ceiling.

Photo courtesy of Armstrong Ceilings

Create a patina effect by randomly dabbing the tiles with metallic green or blue paint, using a natural sea sponge.

Photo courtesy of Armstrong Ceilings

How to Install Ceiling Tile

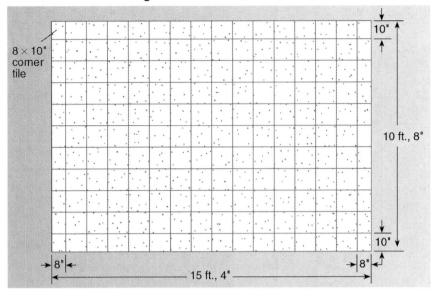

8 × 10" corner tile

10"

10 ft., 8"

10"

8"   8"

15 ft., 4"

1 Measure the distance from wall to wall in the room. If the length comes out in even feet, you do not need to cut border tiles in that direction. If the length does not come out in even feet, use this simple formula to determine the width of the border tiles: add 12 to the number of inches remaining and divide by 2. The result is the width of the border tile. (For example, if the room length is 15 ft., 4", add 12 to the 4, then divide 16 by 2, which results in an 8" border tile width.) Repeat this measurement for the other room dimension.

2 Install the first furring strip flush against the wall at a right angle to the joists. Fasten the strip with two 8d nails or 2" screws at each joist. Measure a distance equal to the border tile width minus ¾" from the wall and snap a chalk line. Install the second furring strip with its wall-side edge aligned along the chalk line.

3 The remaining strips should be installed 12" on center from the second strip. Measure from the second strip and mark the joist nearest the wall every 12". Repeat along the joist on the opposite side of the room, then snap chalk lines between the marks. Install the furring strips along the lines. Install the last furring strip flush against the opposite side wall. Make sure to stagger the butted ends of adjacent strips to avoid falling on the same joist.

4 When all strips are in place, check the level of the strips with a 4-ft. level. Insert wood shims between the strips and joists as necessary to bring the furring strips into a level plane.

5 Establish square string lines along two adjacent walls to keep your installation in line. Inset the strings from the wall by a distance that equals that wall's border tile width plus ½". Use a framing square to check the strings for square. Adjust one string until the strings are perfectly square.

6 Cut the corner border tile to size with a sharp utility knife and straightedge. Cutting the border tiles ¼" short will ease fitting the tiles. The resulting gap between the tile and wall will be covered by the trim molding. Be sure to cut only on the edges without the stapling flange.

7 Put the corner tile into place with the flange edges lined up along the two string lines. Using ½" staples, fasten the tile to the furring strips with four staples. Cut and install two border tiles along each wall, making sure the tiles fit snugly together.

8 Fill in between the border tiles with full-size tiles. Continue working diagonally in this way across to the opposite corner. For the border tiles along the far wall, you'll need to trim off the flange edge; with these tiles, staple through the face of the tile, close to the wall.

9 Install the final row of tiles, saving the far corner tile and the tile next to it for last. Cut and install the corner tile. Cut the last tile to size, then remove the tongue and nailing flange along the side edges to make insertion possible. Finish the installation by nailing decorative ceiling trim along the edges (see pages 20-25).

Tiling a Kitchen Backsplash

There are few spaces in your home with as much potential for creativity and visual impact as the 18" between your kitchen countertop and cupboards. A well designed backsplash can transform your ordinary kitchen into something extraordinary.

While there are many possible materials available for your backsplash, ceramic tile is still a widely popular choice due to its cost, ease of maintenance, and wide variety of colors, textures, and patterns that allow for creativity and personalization.

Tiles for the backsplash can be attached directly to wallboard or plaster and do not require a backerboard. When purchasing the tile, order 10% extra to cover breakage and cutting. Before installing, prepare the work area by removing switch and receptacle coverplates. Protect the countertop from scratches by covering it with a drop cloth.

© Karen Melvin

Everything You Need

Tools: Level, tape measure, pencil, tile cutter, rod saw, notched trowel, rubber grout float, beating block, rubber mallet, sponge, bucket.

Materials: Straight 1 × 2, wall tile, tile spacers (if needed), bullnose trim tile, mastic tile adhesive, masking tape, tile grout, caulk, drop cloth.

Tips for Planning Tile Layouts

Use planning brochures and design catalogs to help create decorative patterns and borders for your backsplash project.

Photo courtesy of Hi-Ho Industries, Inc.

Create a mosaic pattern by breaking tiles into fragments. Always use a sanded grout for joints wider than ⅛".

Photo courtesy of Laufen Ceramic Tile

Painted mural tiles create a charming focal point to the backspash. Mixing various tile styles adds an appealing contrast.

Tips for Cutting Tile

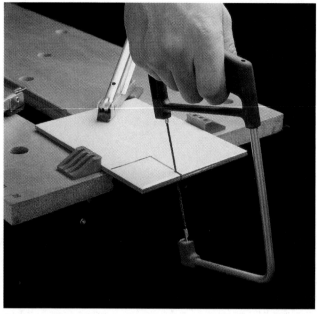

Use a tile cutter to make straight cuts for end pieces. Place the tile face up on the cutter with one side flush against the cutting guide. Adjust the cutting tool to the desired width, and then score a groove by pulling the cutting wheel firmly along the tile. Snap the tile along the scored line, as directed by the tool manufacturer.

Make notches and curved cuts in tile by clamping the tile to a flat surface, then cutting it with a rod saw.

How to Install a Ceramic Tile Backsplash

1 Make a jury stick by marking a board at least half as long as the backsplash area to match the tile spacing (inset). Starting at the midpoint of the installation area, use the jury stick to make layout marks along the wall. If an end piece is too small (less than half a tile), adjust the midpoint to give you larger, more attractive end pieces. Use a level to mark this point with a vertical reference line.

2 While it may appear straight, your countertop may not be level and therefore is not a reliable reference line. Run a level along the counter to find the lowest point on the countertop. Mark a point two tiles up from the low point and extend a level line across the entire work area.

(continued next page)

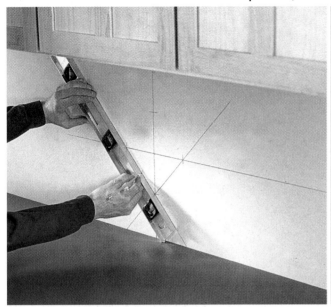

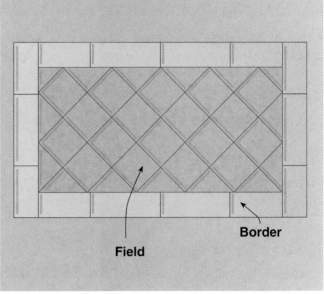

Field

Border

Variation: _Diagonal Layout._ Mark vertical and horizontal reference lines, making sure the angle is 90°. To establish diagonal layout lines, measure out equal distances from the crosspoint, then connect the points with a line. Additonal layout lines can be extended from these as needed. To avoid the numerous, unattractive perimeter cuts common to diagonal layouts, try using a standard border pattern as shown. Diagonally set a field of full tiles only, then cut enough half tiles to fill out the perimeter. Finally, border the diagonal field with tiles set square to the field.

3 Apply mastic adhesive evenly to the area beneath the horizontal reference line, using a notched trowel. Comb the adhesive horizontally with the notched edge.

4 Starting at the vertical reference line, press tiles into the adhesive with a slight twisting motion. If the tiles are not self-spacing, use plastic spacers to maintain even grout lines. If the tiles do not hang in place, use masking tape to hold them in place until the adhesive sets.

5 Install a whole row along the reference line, checking occasionally to make sure the tiles are level. Continue installing tiles below the first row, trimming tiles that butt against the countertop as needed (see page 33).

6 Apply adhesive to an area above the line and continue placing tiles, working from the center to the sides. Install trim tile, such as bullnose tile, to the edges of the rows.

7 When the tiles are in place, make sure they are flat and firmly embedded by laying a beating block against the tile and rapping it lightly with a mallet. Remove the spacers. Allow the mastic to dry for at least 24 hours, or as directed by the manufacturer.

8 Mix the grout and apply it with a rubber grout float. Spread it over the tiles, keeping the float at a low 30° angle, pressing the grout deep into the joints. NOTE: for grout joints ⅛" and smaller, be sure to use a non-sanded grout.

9 Wipe off excess grout, holding the float at a right angle to the tile, working diagonally so as not to remove grout from the joints. Clean any remaining grout from the tiles with a damp sponge, working in a circular motion. Rinse the sponge thoroughly and often.

10 Shape the grout joints by making slow, short, passes with the sponge, shaving down any high spots; rinse the sponge frequently. Fill any voids with a fingerful of grout. When the grout has dried to a haze, buff the tile clean with a soft cloth. Apply a bead of caulk between the countertop and tiles. Reinstall any electrical fixtures you removed. After the grout has completely cured, you may want to apply a grout sealer to help prevent discoloration.

Lighting & Utilities

Installing Incandescent Light Fixtures

Installing new incandescent light fixtures is one of the very best and easiest ways to give your rooms a facelift. Specialty lighting stores and the lighting departments of large home improvement centers have hundreds of wall-hung sconces, ceiling-hung globe fixtures, and chandeliers to choose from.

You will need to understand how to shut off the power to the circuit (see page 44, step 1), but past this, installation couldn't be easier. In most cases, it's simply a matter of connecting the wire leads on the light fixture to the circuit wires of the same color, using twist-style wire connectors.

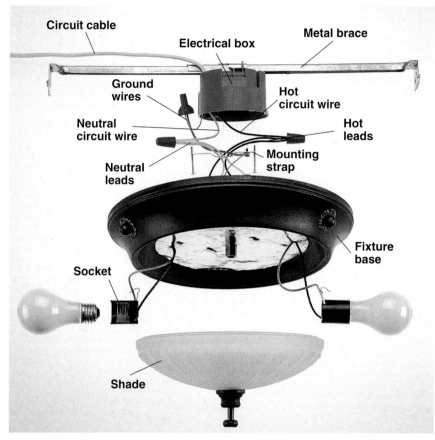

Incandescent light fixtures have preattached wire leads that connect to the house circuit with pre-installed wire leads. Fixtures are secured directly to electrical boxes or to mounting straps attached to the boxes.

Installation Overview: Incandescent Light Fixture

1 Shut off the power and remove the old light fixture. Attach a fixture mounting strap to the electrical box, if the box does not already have one. The strap may have a preinstalled grounding screw.

2 Using wire connectors, connect the white wire lead to the white circuit wire, and the black lead to the black circuit wire. Attach the ground wire to the grounding screw on the mounting strap.

3 Attach the fixture base to the mounting strap, using the screws provided. Install a light bulb with a wattage rating consistent with the fixture rating, then attach the fixture globe.

Installing Track Lighting

Track lights give you the ability to precisely aim ceiling- or wall-mounted light fixtures for a variety of aesthetic effects and practical benefits. In a living room, for example, track lights can highlight artwork, or favorite room accessories. In a kitchen, track lights can illuminate work areas and dining spaces.

It's an easy matter to replace an ordinary ceiling-mounted fixture with a surface-mounted lighting track that connects to the existing electrical box. Additional tracks can be added to the first, using L-connectors or T-connectors. The individual lighting fixtures, available in a variety of styles, can be positioned anywhere along the tracks. You can redesign your lighting scheme whenever you change the look of the room.

Track lighting makes it easy to create custom lighting effects. The individual fixtures can be arranged to highlight art work, provide focused task lighting, or supply indirect lighting to brighten a dark corner.

Installation Overview: Track Lighting

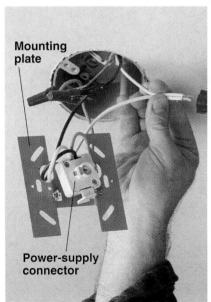

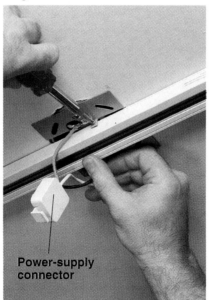

1 Connect the power-supply connector to the circuit wires, using wire connectors. Then, attach the mounting plate to the electrical box.

2 Mount the first track to the ceiling, screwing it into framing members or using toggle bolts. Secure the track to the mounting plate with screws. Snap the power-supply connector into the track.

3 Install additional tracks, connecting them to the first track with L- or T-connectors. Install the power-supply cover. Cap bare track ends with dead-end pieces. Position the light fixtures as desired.

Installing Under-cabinet Lighting

Whether you are looking to add task lighting to a kitchen, office, or shop workspace, or you simply want to give a decorative accent to display shelving, there are a variety of lighting options to meet your needs. Under-cabinet lights come in numerous styles, including mini-track lights, strip lights, halogen puck lights, flexible rope lights (see pages 42-43), and fluorescent task lights (covered here). Because each system has its own distinct lighting qualities, it's best to compare displays at the store to determine which best meets your needs.

Some under-cabinet lighting systems plug into a standard receptacle, while others are designed to be hard-wired into your home's existing circuit, as shown here. This installation shows hard-wiring a series of fluorescent undercabinet lights and installing a new wall switch control.

Consult your electrical inspector about code requirements regarding the type of cable required (some may require armored cable) and the power source from which you draw. Some codes may not allow you to draw power from a receptacle as shown in this project. Also make sure the wattage of the new lights does not exceed the safe capacity of the circuit (see page 50).

Everything You Need

Tools: Neon circuit tester, utility knife, wallboard saw, hammer, screwdriver, drill and hole saw, jig saw, wire stripper.

Materials: Under-cabinet lighting kit, 12-2 NM cable, pigtail wiring, twist-on wire connectors, plastic switch box, switch.

How to Hard-wire Under-cabinet Lighting

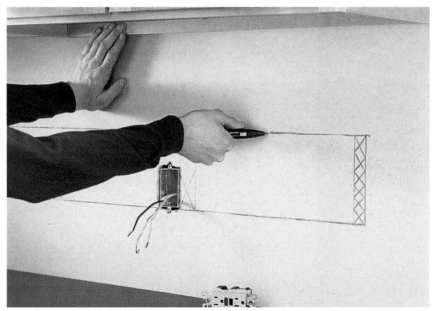

1 Shut off the power to the receptacle you plan to draw power from, then use a neon circuit tester to confirm the power is off (see page 50). Disconnect the receptacle from its wiring. Locate and mark the studs in the installation area. Mark and cut a channel to route the cable, using a utility knife. In order to ease repair of the wallboard when finished, we cut a 6"-tall channel in the center of the installation area.

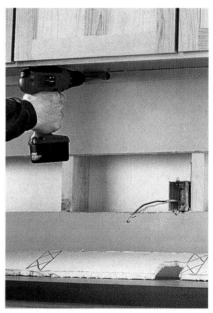

2 Drill holes through the cabinet edging and/or wall surface directly beneath the cabinets where the cable will enter each light fixture. Drill ⅝" holes through the studs to run the cable.

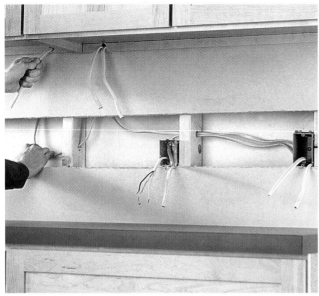

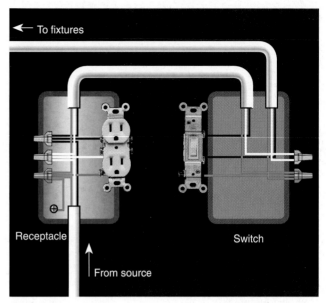

To fixtures ←

Receptacle

Switch

↑ From source

3 Install a plastic switch box by nailing it to the stud with preinstalled nails. Route a piece of 12-2 cable from the switch location to the power source. Route another cable from the switch to the first fixture hole. If you are installing more than one set of lights, route cables from the first fixture location to the second, and so on.

4 Strip 8" of sheathing from the ends of the switch-to-power cable. Clamp the cable into the receptacle box. Using plastic wire connectors, pigtail the white wires to the silver terminal on the receptacle and the black wires to the brass terminal (see page 51). Pigtail the grounding wires to the grounding screw in the electrical box. Tuck wiring into the electrical box and reattach the receptacle.

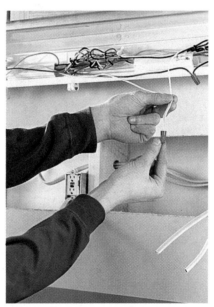

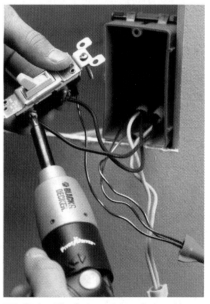

5 Remove the access cover, lens, and bulb from the light fixture. Open the knockouts for running cables into the fixture. Insert the cables into the knockouts and secure the clamps. Strip 8" of sheathing from the cables. Attach the light fixture to the bottom of the cabinet with screws.

6 Use wire connectors to join the black, white, and ground leads from the light fixture to each of the corresponding cable wires from the wall, including any cable leading to additional fixtures. Reattach the bulb, lens and access cover to the fixture. Install any additional fixtures.

7 Strip 8" of sheathing from the two cable ends at the switch and clamp the cables into the switch box. Join the white wires together with wire connectors. Connect each black wire to a screw terminal on the switch. Pigtail the ground wires to the grounding screw on the switch. Install the switch and coverplate; restore power. Patch any removed wallboard (see page 115).

Installing Crown Molding Lighting

Flexible, low-voltage rope lights hidden above a crown molding create a soft, comforting light effect that is much more relaxing than direct lighting. When combined with light colored walls and ceilings, this system provides cool, balanced lighting, with no eye-straining glare. A stand-alone run along a wall can be used to draw attention to a room's focal point.

Rope lights can be easily adapted to any length of lighting run. Connect one rope to another by simply removing the end caps and inserting male/female connectors into the ends. You can also trim rope lighting to length at marked cutting lines located every 18".

Everything You Need

Tools: Stud finder, pencil, chalk line, drill, tape measure, bevel gauge, table saw or circular saw, miter saw, square, jig saw, hammer, nail set.

Materials: Crown molding, rope lighting, 2 × 2 lumber, 3" wallboard screws, 6d finish nails, mounting clips for rope lighting (optional).

How to Install Crown Molding Lighting

1 Use a stud finder to locate studs in the installation area. Mark the stud locations with light pencil marks near the ceiling, making sure the lines will be visible when the trim is in place. Plan the layout order of the molding pieces so as to minimize cuts and avoid noticeable joints (see page 21). Also keep in mind the location of the receptacle that you plan to plug the rope lighting into.

3" to 12"

2 Determine the location for your molding. To maximize light reflection from the walls and ceiling, position the molding 3" to 12" from the ceiling. Measure from the ceiling and mark a point to represent the bottom edge of the molding. Mark at the ends of each wall that you plan to work on, then snap a chalk line between the marks.

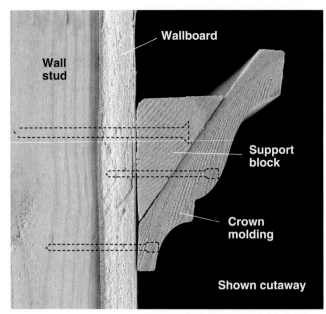

Wall stud

Wallboard

Support block

Crown molding

Shown cutaway

3 Because the crown molding will not be fastened at the top, it is necessary to install support blocking. Use a bevel gauge to determine the precise angle of your crown molding. Rip 2 × 2 lumber to this angle, using a table saw or circular saw. Fasten the supports to wall studs using 3" screws. The supports can be installed in long strips or cut into 6" blocks and attached at each molding joint and every 4 ft. on long runs of molding.

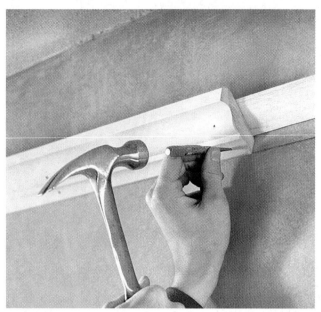

4 Set the molding in place along the chalk line. Have a helper hold the molding in place as you drill pilot holes and fasten it with 6d finish nails. Drive one nail into the stud along the lower edge of the molding and one into the support blocking. Use a nail set to recess the nail heads slightly.

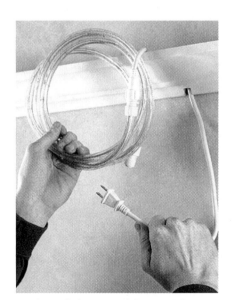

5 Install the remaining sections of molding. When you are above the receptacle you will use to power the rope lighting, cut a small notch in the molding with a jig saw and lay the cord in the notch before fastening the molding to the wall.

6 Follow the manufacturer's instructions to join or cut any segments of rope lighting to the proper length. Lay the rope light in the trough between the wall and molding and work it around the entire installation. You may want to use mounting clips (sold separately) to keep the rope lighting lying flat. Plug in the light to activate it.

Variation: Flip the molding upside down and attach it to the wall for a cornice lighting effect. Attach the rope lighting to the top of the cornice with mounting clips sold separately by the manufacturer.

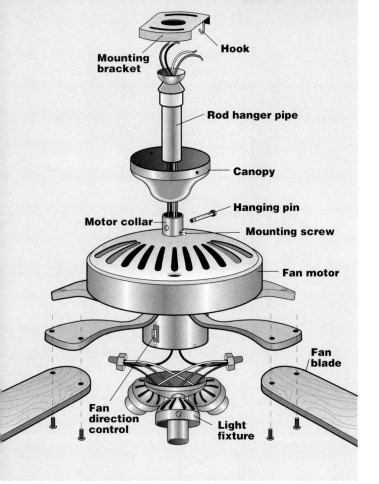

Mounting bracket

Hook

Rod hanger pipe

Canopy

Hanging pin

Motor collar

Mounting screw

Fan motor

Fan blade

Fan direction control

Light fixture

Installing a Ceiling Fan-light

A combination fan-light is one of the best choices you can make for a ceiling fixture. In warm months, its cooling breeze can make a room comfortable, and in winter, when run at low speeds, it can also circulate warm air down from the ceiling. Using the wiring from an existing light fixture, you can easily install your own ceiling fan-light.

Most standard ceiling fans work with a wall switch functioning as master power for the unit. Pull chains attached to the unit control the fan and lights. If you would like to eliminate the pull chains, consider installing a remote control device that gives you hand-held control of fan speed and light brightness. Some fans come equipped with these remote units, or they may be purchased separately.

Everything You Need

Tools: Stepladder, screwdrivers (Phillips and flat-head), wire stripper, pliers or adjustable wrench, neon circuit tester, hammer.

Materials: Ceiling fan-light kit, 2 × 4 lumber or adjustable ceiling fan cross brace, 1½" and 3" wall-board screws.

How to Install a Ceiling Fan-light

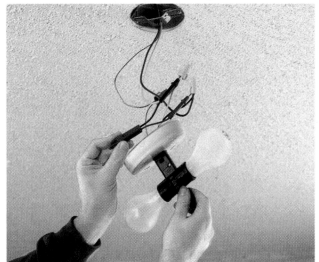

1 Shut off the power to the circuit at the service panel. Unscrew the existing fixture and carefully pull it away from the ceiling. Do not touch bare wires. Use a neon circuit tester to make sure the power is off by inserting the probes into the wire connectors on the black and white wires. If the tester lights, return to the service panel and turn off the correct circuit. If the tester does not light, disconnect the wire connectors and remove the old fixture.

2 Due to the added weight and vibration of a ceiling fan, you must determine whether the existing electrical box will provide adequate support. If you can access the box from the attic, check to see that it is a metal, not plastic, box and that it has a heavy-duty cross brace rated for ceiling fans. If the box is not adequately braced, cut a 2 × 4 to fit between the joists and attach it with 3" screws. Attach a metal electrical box to the brace from below with at least three 1½" wallboard screws. Attach the fan mounting bracket to the box.

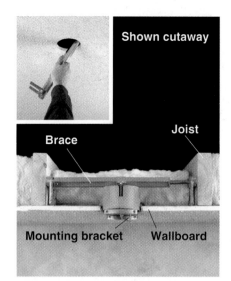

Shown cutaway

Brace   Joist

Mounting bracket   Wallboard

Variation: If the joists are inaccessible from above, install an adjustable ceiling fan brace through the rough opening in the ceiling. Remove the old box. Insert the fan brace through the hole, adjust until it fits tightly between the joists, then attach the box with the included hardware. Make sure the lip of the box is flush with the ceiling wallboard before attaching the mounting bracket.

Rod hanger pipe   Canopy

3 Run the wires from the top of the fan motor through the canopy and then through the rod hanger pipe. Slide the rod hanger pipe through the canopy and attach the pipe to the motor collar using the included hanging pin. Tighten the mounting screws firmly.

Hanging pin

4 Hang the motor assembly by the hook on the mounting bracket. Connect the wires according the manufacturer's directions, using wire connectors to join the fixture wires to the circuit wires in the box. Gather the wires together and tuck them inside the fan canopy. Lift the canopy and attach it to the mounting bracket.

Wires to fan motor and light

Remote control receiver

Wires to house circuit

Variation: *Remote Control.* To install a remote control, fit the receiver inside the fan canopy. Follow the manufacturer's wiring diagram to wire the unit. The receiver will have a set of three wires that connects to the corresponding wires from the fan motor and lights, and another set that connects to the two circuit wires from the electrical box.

5 Attach the fan blades one at a time with the included hardware. Follow the manufacturer's directions.

Fan housing

6 Connect the wiring for the fan's light fixture according to the manufacturer's directions. Tuck all wires into the switch housing and attach the fixture. Install light bulbs and globes. Restore power and test the fan. If the fan vibrates excessively, check the manufacturer's documentation to adjust the balance. If the fan doesn't run at all, turn off the power and check the wiring connections.

Building Custom Light Boxes

Basements can be difficult to light adequately, because the ceilings are too low for many light fixtures. These light boxes provide a perfect solution. They fit between ceiling joists, and can be sized to hold 2-, 4-, or 6-ft. light fixtures.

Here's how a light box is made: Two pieces of blocking are installed between two floor joists to form the box (see page 47). The wiring is run from a wall switch into the box, then the inside of the box is wrapped with ¼" wallboard. After the wallboard is finished and painted, one fluorescent light fixture is installed on each long side of the box, and the wiring connections are made. Then, a piece of crown molding and a spacer are cut to length to fit under each fixture. Reflective tape is applied to the back of the molding, and the molding and spacers are painted and fastened to the box sides.

Part of the planning for building a light box is finding an effective combination of molding and spacer pieces. The molding must project far enough from the box side so that it conceals the fixture from view but allows enough room for changing the lamp. A spacer cut from standard 2 × lumber combined with

a 5" or 6" crown molding should provide the desired effect.

The wiring diagrams on page 47 show you a fixture connection and the basic wiring layout for multiple light boxes. If you're not familiar with basic wiring techniques and installation, hire an electrician to rough-in the wiring and make the final connections for your light boxes. Be sure to have all of the electrical work approved by a building inspector.

Everything You Need:

Tools: Combination square, circular saw, drill, wallboard knives, paintbrush, nail set, caulk gun.

Materials: 2 × lumber, 3" wallboard screws, 14/2 NM cable, cable staples, single-pole light switch, electrical box, wire connectors, fluorescent light fixtures, ¼" wallboard, corner bead, wallboard tape and compound, paint, crown molding, foil duct tape, finish nails, caulk, wood putty.

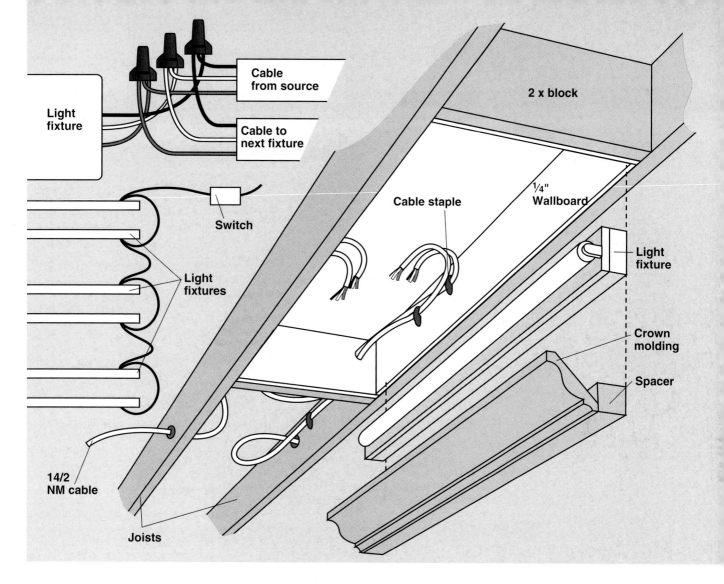

Light fixture

Cable from source

Cable to next fixture

2 x block

Switch

Cable staple

1/4" Wallboard

Light fixtures

Light fixture

Crown molding

Spacer

14/2 NM cable

Joists

How to Install Light Boxes

1 Mark the box frame locations by making Xs on the bottom edges of the joists. The inside of the frames should be about 2" longer than the light fixtures. Use a combination square to extend the layout lines onto the faces of the joists. Cut each block to fit, using the same size lumber as the joists. Set the blocks along the layout lines, and attach them with 3" wallboard screws. Drill ⅝" holes through the end blocks and run wiring for the boxes (see diagram above).

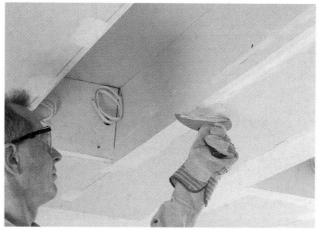

2 Cover all of the surfaces inside the box with ¼" wallboard. Complete the wallboard installation over the main ceiling surface, using ½" or ⅝" wallboard, then finish the outside corners of the box with corner bead. Tape and finish the inside corners of the boxes. Paint the entire surface inside each box with a light-colored, semi-gloss latex paint.

(continued next page)

3 Install the fixtures in each box, positioning them so the lamp will face the center of the box. Center the fixtures from side to side, and fasten them to the joists with screws. Connect the fixture wiring to the circuit cables, following the manufacturer's instructions.

4 Cut the crown molding to fit snugly between the ends of the boxes. Paint the front faces of the molding, using the same paint used inside the boxes. Line the inside surfaces of each piece of molding with reflective foil duct tape.

5 Determine the size of the spacers by positioning a piece of molding under a fixture with a lamp installed. Hold the molding away from the box side until you find the desired position. Then, measure between the molding and the box side to find the width of the spacer. Cut the spacer to width from 2 × lumber. Drill pilot holes for screws through the front edge of each spacer, then sand and paint spacers to match molding.

6 Attach the spacers inside the boxes with wallboard screws. Make sure all spacers are level and at the same height. Attach the crown molding pieces to the front edges of the spacers with finish nails driven through pilot holes. Set the nails with a nail set, and fill the holes with wood putty. Seal any gaps at the ends of the molding with paintable caulk, then touch-up the paint on the joints and nail holes.

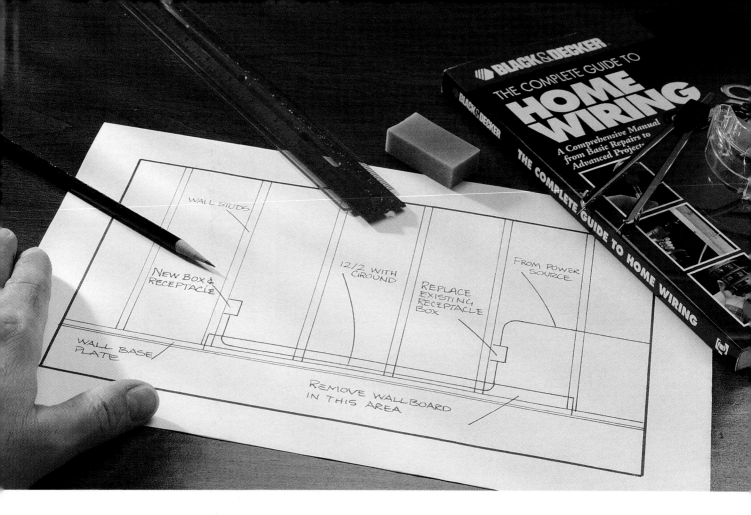

The image shows a hand-drawn wiring diagram with the following labels: "WALL STUDS", "NEW BOX & RECEPTACLE", "12/2 WITH GROUND", "REPLACE EXISTING RECEPTACLE BOX", "FROM POWER SOURCE", "WALL BASE PLATE", "REMOVE WALLBOARD IN THIS AREA". Also visible is a book titled "BLACK & DECKER — THE COMPLETE GUIDE TO HOME WIRING — A Comprehensive Manual from Basic Repairs to Advanced Projects."

Adding a New Receptacle

Homes built before 1970 or so are likely to have fewer electrical receptacles than are adequate to meet the needs of today's appliances and home electronics. One might find that a new furniture layout suddenly places lamps in awkward positions or with cords stretched their distance. Or perhaps the new family computer would fit perfectly in the corner of a family room, but it requires an extension cord to reach the nearest receptacle. Octopus receptacle expanders and extension cords can be temporary fixes, but are both unsightly and potentially dangerous. With some basic tools and an eye on safety, you can add new receptacles to your home wherever your lifestyle demands power.

Everything You Need

Tools: Neon circuit tester, pencil, jig saw or wallboard saw, reciprocating saw with metal-cutting blade, cable ripper, utility knife, combination tool, needlenose pliers, fish tape, drill with ⅝" bit, drill bit extender.

Materials: Retrofit electrical boxes, 12-2 NM cable, standard receptacle, metal nail plates, string, electrical tape, twist-on wire connectors.

The easiest way to install a new receptacle is to tap into the circuit from an existing receptacle, as shown in this project. Depending upon the wiring configuration, you might also be able to tap into a switch, light fixture box, or junction box in the basement or attic. Remember, wherever you place the new outlet, you will have to run cable through the wall studs, or through the floor or ceiling.

Begin by planning the receptacle location and the most direct route to a connecting circuit. The best placement will be along the same wall as an existing receptacle. As you are planning, also consider the location of hidden utilities, such as plumbing lines, gas pipes, ductwork, or wiring, before you make any cuts into walls, floors, or ceilings.

Before adding a receptacle, you'll need to map the connecting circuit and evaluate its safe capacity. Safe capacity is the total amount of power the circuit wires can reliably carry without tripping the circuit breaker or blowing a fuse. The demand for power must not exceed the safe capacity of the circuit. Also, make sure the new receptacle has the same amperage and voltage ratings as the circuit.

How to Evaluate the Circuit

  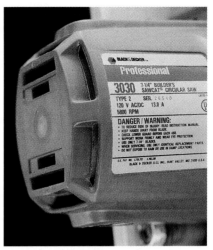

1 First determine the amperage and voltage ratings of the circuit. Amperage should be listed on the breaker or rim of the fuse. Voltage is either 120 or 240 (high voltage). Do not install a regular receptacle on a high-voltage circuit. Multiply amps times volts to find the total capacity of the circuit in watts. Safe capacity is listed in step 4.

2 Turn off the power at the main breakers. Turn on only the circuit with the existing receptacle you hope to tap into. If your service box is not labeled, you may need some trial and error to find the correct circuit. Use a neon circuit tester to determine all the receptacles and fixtures controlled by that circuit.

3 To find the demand of the circuit, add the wattage ratings for all lights and appliances on the circuit. Add the wattages of all the lightbulbs in a fixture to find its total wattage. Wattage ratings for appliances are often listed on the manufacturer's label. Approximate wattage ratings for some common appliances are given below.

Safe Capacity of Circuits

Amps x Volts	Total Capacity	Safe Capacity
15A x 120V	1800 watts	1440 watts
20A x 120V	2400 watts	1920 watts
25A x 120V	3000 watts	2400 watts
30A x 120V	3600 watts	2880 watts

Common Wattage Ratings

Appliance	Watts
Blender	240-480
Computer	480-840
Ceiling Fan	420
Coffee Maker	480-960
Color Television	300
Dishwasher	1020-1500
DVD Player	300-480
Frying Pan	1080
Garbage Disposal	420-900
Hair Dryer	600-1200
Microwave Oven	1000-1500
Portable Heater	840-1440
Refrigerator	240-600
Stereo	300-480
Toaster	1080
Vacuum Cleaner	720-1320

Amps: 20

Volts: 120

Total capacity (watts): 2400

Safe capacity (watts): 1920

Appliance/Fixture	Watts
CEILING FAN	420
TELEVISION	300
STEREO	400
TABLE LAMP (2 60-WATT BULBS)	120
Present Demand	1240
+ New Demand	
COMPUTER	600
Total Demand	1840

4 Once you have evaluated the existing demand upon the circuit, add the expected wattage demand of the new service. If the total wattage demand exceeds the safe capacity of the circuit (above), call an electrician and install a new circuit. Or, find another circuit from which to draw power.

How to Strip NM Cable & Wires

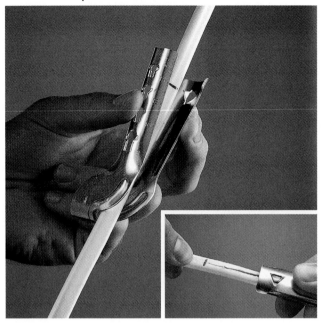

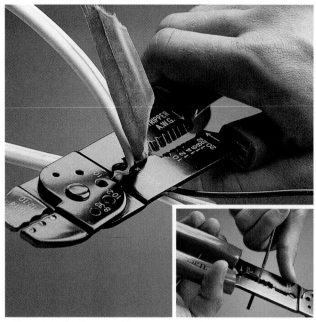

1 Measure and mark the cable 8" to 10" from the end. Slide a cable ripper onto the cable, and squeeze the tool firmly to force the cutting point through the plastic sheathing. Pull the cable ripper toward the end of the cable to cut open the plastic sheathing (inset).

2 Cut away the excess sheathing and paper wrapping using the cutting jaws of a combination tool or a utility knife. Strip ¾" insulation from each wire, using the stripper openings (inset). Choose the opening that matches the gauge of the wire, and take care not to nick or scratch the ends of the wires.

How to Connect Wires to Screw Terminals

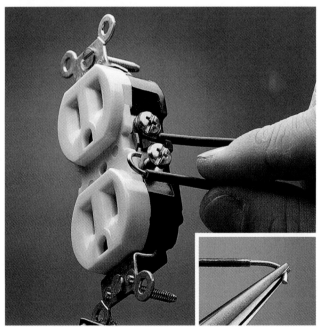

Connect wires to screw terminals on receptacles and switches by forming a C-shaped loop on the end of each wire, using a needlenose pliers (inset). Hook each wire around a screw terminal so it forms a clockwise loop. Tighten the screw firmly. The wire insulation should just touch the head of the screw. Never attach two wires to a single screw terminal. Instead, use a pigtail wire (right).

How to Pigtail Wires

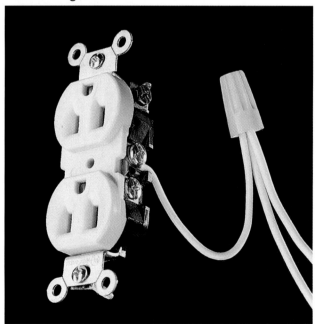

Connect two or more wires to a single terminal with a pigtail. A pigtail is a short piece of wire. Connect one end of the pigtail to a screw terminal, and the other end to the circuit wires, using a wire connector. NOTE: The pigtail must be of the same type and gauge as the circuit wires.

How to Install a New Receptacle

1 Once you know the circuit you wish to extend can support the new service without overloading the circuit, position the new box on the wall, and trace around it. Consider the location of hidden utilities within the wall before you cut. Carefully cut out the hole pattern with a jig saw or wallboard saw. The box should fit snugly into the hole.

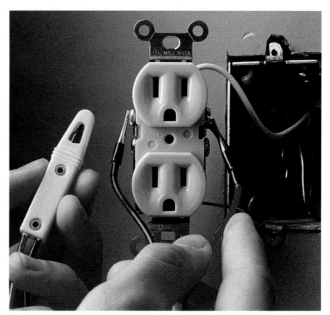

2 Shut off power at the service panel. Test the receptacle from which you will draw power, using a neon circuit tester. If tester does not glow, pull out the receptacle from its electrical box, still being careful not to touch any wires. Test the receptacle again, by placing one probe to the brass screw terminal and one probe to the silver screw terminal. If the tester doesn't glow, the wires are safe to handle.

3 Disconnect and remove the receptacle from the box. Examine the box to determine how it was installed. Most older metal boxes are attached to framing members with nails or metal mounting straps. Cut through the nails or straps using a reciprocating saw equipped with a metal cutting blade, taking care not to damage any of the circuit wires.

4 To prevent the wires from falling in, gather the wires from each cable and tie each with string, securing the string with electrical tape. Disconnect the locknuts or internal clamps and pull out the old electrical box, making sure wires do not fall into the wall cavity.

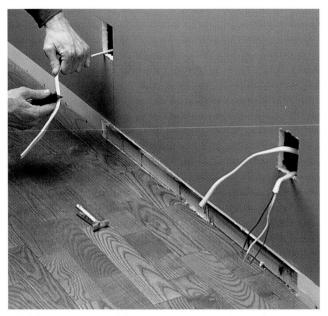

5 Route the cable between the new and old holes. This will require removing wall material and drilling holes through framing members to route the cable through (see page 54 for options for running cable). Once routed, strip the cable sheathing from about 8" of cable.

6 Thread the new and old cables into a retrofit box large enough to contain the added wires and clamp the cables. Fit the box into the old hole and attach it with the included screws.

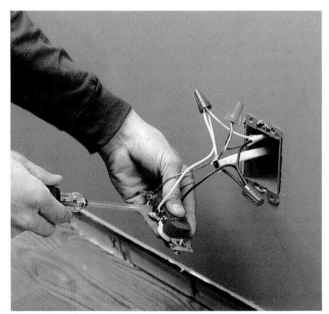

7 Use short pieces of wire and twist-on wire connectors to pigtail the new and old wiring to the existing receptacle. Pigtail the white (neutral) wires to the silver terminal and the black (hot) wires to the brass terminal on the receptacle; pigtail the green ground wires to the grounding screw on the receptacle. Push the receptacle and all wiring back into electrical box, then reattach the receptacle and coverplate.

8 Pull the cable through the retrofit box for the new receptacle, leaving about 10" out, and clamp it. Insert and secure the new box into the new hole. Connect the new receptacle to the new circuit cable. Connect the white wire to the silver terminal, the black wire to the brass terminal and the ground wire to the grounding screw on the receptacle. Insert the wiring into the box and attach the receptacle and coverplate.

How to Run Cable Along a Baseboard

1 Remove baseboard between new and existing receptacle. Cut away the wall material about 1" below the baseboard with a jig saw, wallboard saw, or utility knife.

2 Drill a ⅝" hole in the center of each stud along the opening between the two receptacles. A drill bit extender will allow you a better angle and make drilling the holes easier.

3 Run cable through the holes. Staple the cable to the stud before it enters the box. Install a metal nail plate on the front edge of each stud that the cable routes through. Patch the wall material or install ½"-thick wood strips. Reattach the baseboard by nailing it to the studs.

Tips for Running Cable Into a Basement or Attic

You may find it necessary to route cable vertically through a wall, if, for example, you are tapping into a basement junction box or routing cable through an attic to an opposite wall. In either a basement or attic, look for reference points, such as plumbing or electrical cables that indicate the location of the wall. Drill a 1" hole into the stud cavity.

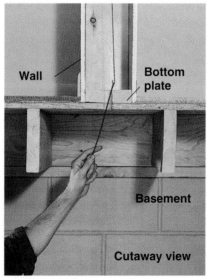

When running cable into a basement, extend a fish tape through the new receptacle hole into the stud cavity. Hook the fish tape from below with a piece of stiff wire and pull it into the basement. Bind the cable to the fish tape with electrical tape and pull the cable up through the hole.

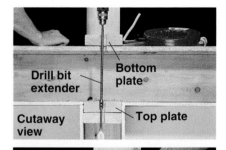

When running cable into an attic, drill a 1" hole down through the top plate and into the stud cavity, using a drill bit extender (top). Extend a fish tape down into the stud cavity, bind the cable to the fish tape, and draw the cable up into the attic (bottom).

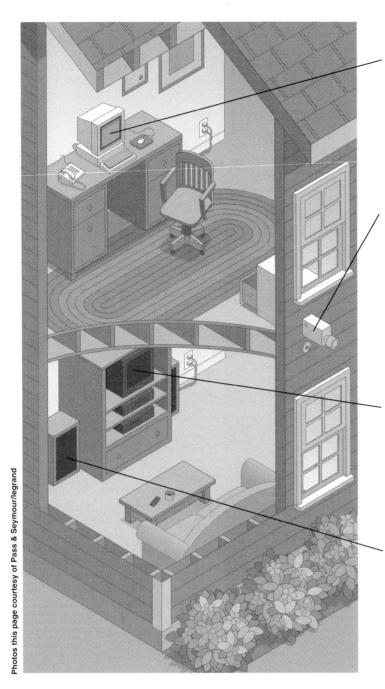

Voice/data (RJ45) jacks can accept any pin-size telecommunication jack, including standard phone and data lines, as well as multi-line computer data connections for a home office.

Accessories, such as closed-circuit cameras, allows homeowners to tailor a system to their specific needs.

Video (F-connector) jacks provide connections for receiving and redistributing TV, VCR, DVD, and closed-circuit camera signals.

Audio terminals or a recessed speaker system can enhance a home theater system or be used to create a whole-house audio system with localized volume control.

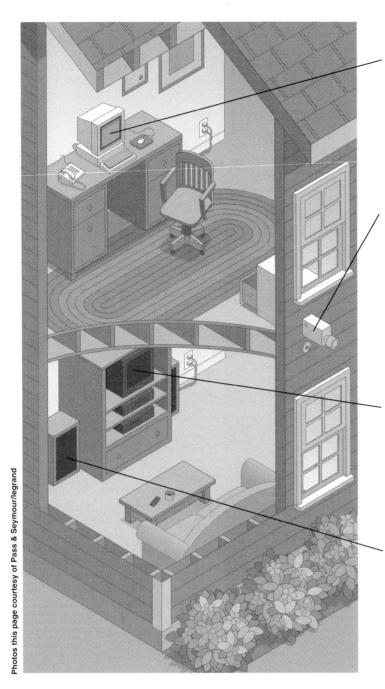

Photos this page courtesy of Pass & Seymour/legrand

Networking Your Home

A network system that links all the major electronics in your home—telephones, computers, cable television, DVD video, intercoms, stereo sound and security systems—can simplify the operation of these systems.

With simple plug-in wall jacks and hidden wiring leading to a central distribution center, a home network system allows every room to be a full-featured multi-media center. Up to now, home networks were only found in newly built homes and were installed at the time of construction. Now, though, there are sev-

eral manufacturers who offer full-line systems that can be retrofitted into existing homes. These products are becoming available at major home improvement centers and are completely suitable for do-it-yourselfers. You can purchase and install the entire system at once or add features over time. The following pages provide an overview of the planning and installation of a basic network system available from Pass & Seymour company.

Planning a Home Network System

Installing a home network system is a project that any homeowner can accomplish. Begin by carefully determining the components your system will require. The whole system revolves around the hub, or *distribution center* (photo A). This is mounted in a basement or a utility closet, and it receives all of the input connections from outside the home, such as phone, internet, and cable or satellite TV lines, as well as stereo and video connections from an entertainment center inside the home. The distribution center contains various *distribution modules* (photo B), each designed to transmit specific voice, data, and video (VDV) signals. Some modules receive electrical power from a receptacle mounted inside the distribution box, allowing them to send strong signals to multiple outlets. From the modules, *high-performance cabling and wire* (photo C) are routed to any room in the house, where they connect to specialty *multimedia outlets* (photo D). The outlets are said to be "plug-and-play," meaning they contain jacks that accept standard plugs for audio/video, computer, phone, and other household equipment.

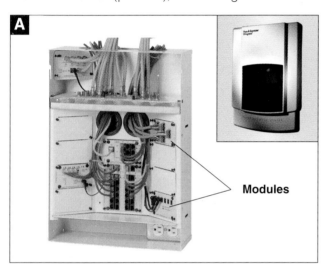

The distribution center houses all of the modules, cable and wire connections, and the power supply for the entire network system. A plastic cover (inset) provides protection and allows easy access to the modules and cable connections, making it easy to reconfigure outlets or make any system changes.

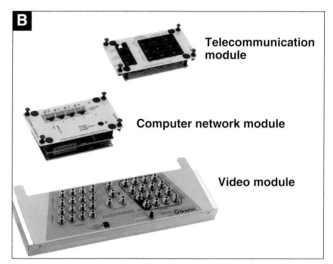

Distribution modules are interface devices that maintain the strength of incoming signals for distribution throughout the system. Modules can also redistribute internal signals to create in-home camera monitoring systems or to route DVD, VCR, or audio signals from a single location to any room in the house.

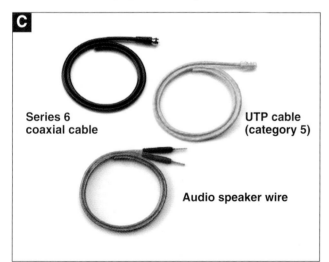

High-performance cabling and wire carry signals between the modules, outlets, and equipment. Series 6 coaxial cable distributes audio/video signals, category 5 cabling carries phone and data signals, and high-grade audio speaker wire routes audio signals throughout the system.

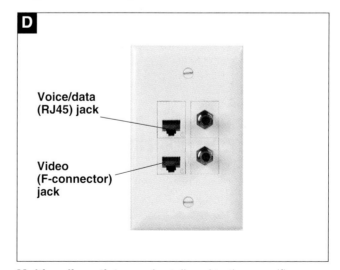

Multimedia outlets can be tailored to the specific needs of each room. Outlets contain a series of jacks and connectors (see page 55) for plug-and-play connection. For convenience, many outlets can be installed next to standard electrical receptacles.

Although it is easier to run cables and wires in the construction phase before the walls are finished, retrofit installations are quite manageable if you carefully plan the system needs, determine the optimal location for each component, and map out the cable and wire routes.

As a general rule, it's a good idea to plan for more cabling and multimedia outlets than you think you will currently use (a teenager's bedroom may become a home office in a few years).

The living room, home office, bedroom, entertainment and recreation rooms, and den are all obvious places for outlets, but outlets in rooms such as the kitchen, bathroom, laundry and utility room, or at locations near large appliances, will help prepare your home for future conveniences and home automation features.

Include multiple outlets in various locations of specific rooms, especially in entertainment areas and the home office. A home office will also benefit from multiple phone and data lines for internet access on the computer. Locate these outlets near receptacles to simplify computer connections.

Sketches and routing maps will help you plan the wire and cable runs. Installing network system lines is similar to running electrical cable. To maximize cable performance, plan the runs with as few turns and bends as possible.

Building Codes

With the increasing need for networking capabilities in the home, standards have been developed by the Telecommunications Industry Association (TIA) and the Electronic Industry Alliance (EIA) in accordance with the Federal Communications Commission (FCC). These standards are becoming the code requirements for home network wiring installation across the country.

Make sure to check with your local building inspector for the current codes in this new and changing area of home wiring.

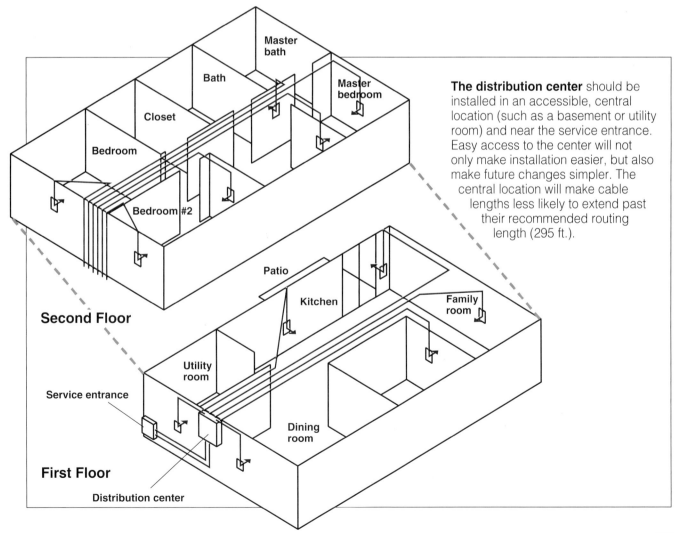

The distribution center should be installed in an accessible, central location (such as a basement or utility room) and near the service entrance. Easy access to the center will not only make installation easier, but also make future changes simpler. The central location will make cable lengths less likely to extend past their recommended routing length (295 ft.).

Preparing Multimedia Outlets

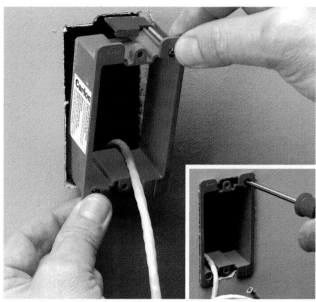

In new construction, use extension brackets to install multimedia outlets next to existing electrical receptacles. Fit the bracket over the receptacle, and fasten it to the stud with screws, then install the new outlet box. Use standard double-gang boxes or hollow-backed boxes (see photo, right) for single outlets—this prevents bending and twisting that can damage the wiring. Mount individual outlet boxes 12" from the floor, measured to the box center.

For retrofit installations, use plastic retrofit boxes (hollow-backed or double-gang). Cut a hole in the wallboard and insert the box, then turn the mounting screws until the ears clamp snugly to the back of the wallboard. Route all wiring to the boxes, leaving at least 12" of slack at each box.

Mounting the Distribution Center

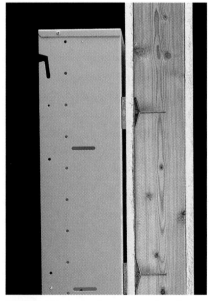

Mount the distribution center at least 48" above the floor, in an easily accessible location. Many units can be recess-mounted between studs with 16" on-center spacing.

Distribution centers can also be surface mounted on finished walls, or attached to a wood backer board. Leave at least ¼" gap between the unit and wall to make it easier to install modules and fasten hardware.

Install a dedicated 15-amp, 120-volt, non-switchable duplex receptacle either in the enclosure itself, or within 60" of the distribution center. A transformer will be used to distribute power to the modules that require it.

Routing Cables & Wires

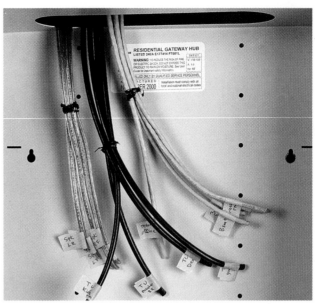

Drill holes in the top plate above the distribution center for routing wiring into the enclosure. Where network wiring runs next to electrical cables in long stretches, maintain a 6" space between them. Feed cables from the outlet locations to the distribution center. See page 54 for tips on installing cable in finished walls and unfinished walls.

Label each run of cable at both the distribution center and the room outlet. At the distribution center, cut each cable to hang even with the bottom of the enclosure. Attach a label with its room location and the specified module connection. At the outlet end of the cable, label it according to its module connection.

Attaching Connectors to Cable Ends

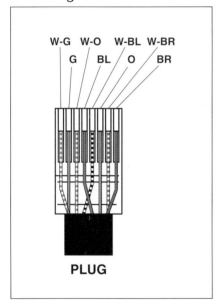

W-G W-O W-BL W-BR
G   BL   O   BR

PLUG

Category 5 cable carries voice and data signals. It contains four twisted pairs of color-coded wires. To attach an RJ45 plug (see photo, right), untwist the wires and arrange them in the plug according to the wiring assignment chart provided by the manufacturer.

Install plugs using a crimping tool. Make sure that each wire is matched to the proper conductor and that ½" of outer insulation is inside the plug, then crimp the plug to secure it.

Use F-connector fittings to connect coaxial cable to F-connector video terminals. Slide the connector over the stripped end of the cable, and attach it with an F-connector crimping tool.

Terminating the Cables

RJ45 jacks are the ports for connecting phone and data devices to the network system. The jacks are wired to a universal pin/pair assignment standard (standard T568A), which allows any size telecommunication plug to be used with the jack. The back side of RJ45 jacks are color-coded to simplify installation. Use a punch-down tool to connect the wires to the terminals, then snap the jack into the outlet (inset).

F-connector terminals, in conjunction with coaxial cables, provide antenna, cable TV, and satellite signals, as well as internal transmission signals from DVDs, VCRs, and closed-circuit cameras. The F-connector fittings on coaxial cable ends are threaded and screw onto the F-connector terminals.

How to Make the Final Connections

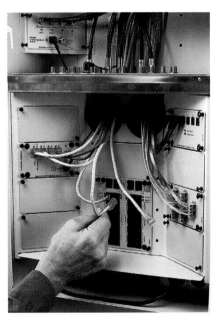

1 Install a mounting bracket (if required) to the distribution center for mounting the various modules. Determine where each module will be placed and route the appropriate cables to their corresponding module.

2 Attach the modules using push-pin grommets or screws. Install a power module to supply modules that require electrical current. A power module connects to a transformer that's plugged into the distribution-center receptacle.

3 Connect the cables to the proper module, using the labels for guidance. Connect cables for incoming service and internal networks to INPUT ports, and those routed to outlets to OUTPUT ports. Finally, test the system, then attach the cover.

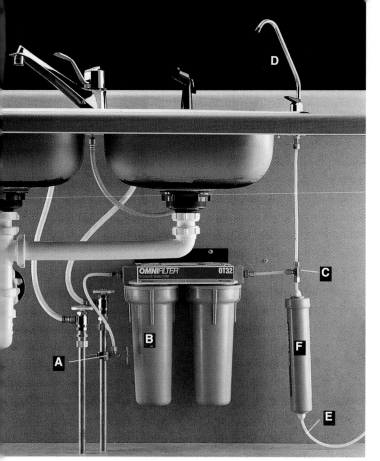

Installing a Water Filtration System

Ensure the water your family uses for drinking and cooking is pure and great tasting by installing a water filtration system. Water filters are effective in reducing lead, chlorine, bacteria, rust, and other contaminants. Undersink systems are typically used to improve the taste of drinking water. Whole-house systems help improve water's taste as well as reduce sediment flowing into your water softener, prolonging its life. Installing both provides the best-tasting and safest water.

Though most systems have similar installation procedures, always follow the manufacturer's instructions. Our undersink installation includes an optional secondary filter that supplies a refrigerator icemaker. This project also shows you how to make the necessary plumbing connections if you choose to install a new icemaker in your refrigerator.

An undersink water filtration system includes a saddle valve (A), filtration unit (B), T-coupling (C), drinking water faucet (D), and refrigerator icemaker line (E). An additional filter (F) for a refrigerator icemaker can be installed.

Everything You Need

Tools: Drill (for faucet), channel-type pliers.

Materials: ¼" flexible vinyl mesh tubing, saddle valve, brass compression fittings, undersink water filter unit, refrigerator icemaker filter and T-coupling (optional).

How to Install an Undersink Water Filtration System

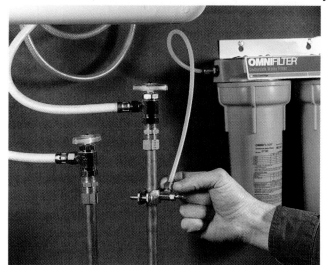

1 Mount the filter unit under the sink, according to manufacturer's directions. Shut off the main water supply, then install a saddle valve on the cold water line, making sure the valve is closed. Connect vinyl mesh tubing from the intake side of the filtration unit to the saddle valve. Attach a vinyl mesh tube to the outtake side of the water filter unit. If you're installing an icemaker filter, attach a T-coupling to the free end of this tube (see photo, top).

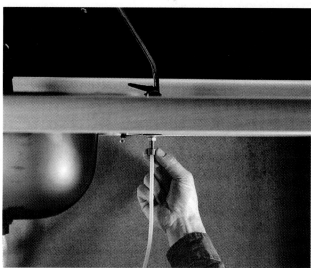

2 Install the drinking water faucet on the countertop, according to manufacturer's directions. Connect a vinyl mesh tube between the faucet tailpiece and the top of the T-coupling (or directly to the water filter, if no icemaker filter is being installed). Attach the icemaker filter to the other outlet on the T-coupling, then run flexible tubing to the icemaker. Turn on the water and open the saddle valve. Inspect all connections for leaks.

Installation Overview: Whole-house Water Filtration System

1 Shut off the main water supply, and drain the pipes. Locate the unit along the supply pipe after the water meter but before any other appliances. Measure and mark the pipe to accommodate the filtration unit as well as a shutoff valve on each side of the filter. Cut the pipe with a pipe cutter. Join the water meter side of pipe with the intake side of unit, and the house supply side of pipe with the outtake side of the unit. Tighten all fittings with a wrench.

2 Install a filter and screw the cover to the bottom of the filtration unit. If your electrical system is grounded through the water pipes, attach a jumper wire to the pipes at each side of unit, using ground clamps. Open the main water supply lines to restore the water supply. Allow faucets to run for a few minutes, as you check to make sure that the system is working properly.

Installation Overview: Connecting a Refrigerator Icemaker

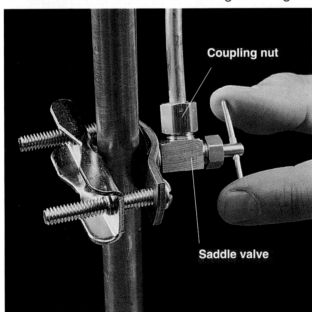

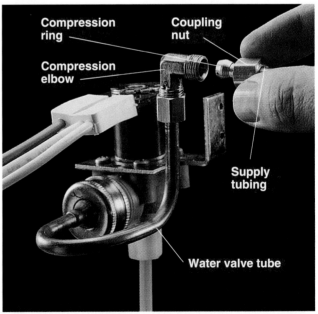

1 Shut off the water at the nearest shutoff valve and drain the nearest cold water pipe. Attach a ¼" saddle valve to the pipe. Connect ¼" soft copper tubing to the saddle valve with a compression ring and coupling nut. Closing the spigot fully causes the spike inside the saddle valve to puncture the water pipe.

2 Run the copper tubing to the refrigerator. Connect the water supply tube to the water valve tube, using a ¼" compression elbow. Slide coupling nuts and compression rings over the tubes, and insert the tubes into the elbow. Tighten the coupling nuts with channel-type pliers. Turn on the water and check all joints for leaks.

Installing a Gas Fireplace

A gas fireplace provides one of the most dramatic upgrades you can make to a room. It's most appropriate to a large living area—a living room, family room, or recreation room—where it brings literal and aesthetic warmth to the communal space.

This project is especially suitable when you are creating new living areas from unfinished space, such as a basement, because you can frame in the fireplace at the same time you are framing and finishing the walls. Or, with just a little bit of ingenuity, you can retrofit an existing finished room with a fireplace.

Today's gas fireplaces are actually fairly easy to install, and many use venting systems that require no elaborate chimney systems. Direct venting is a venti-lation system that uses a special 2-in-1 vent pipe: The inner pipe carries exhaust fumes outside, while the outer pipe draws in fresh air for combustion.

Gas fireplaces are commonly available as standard *(decorative)* or *heater* types. They are similar in appearance, but heater models are designed to provide much more heat to a room. This heat can enter the room passively or be blown into the room by an optional electric fan. Other options for both types include remote starting and electronic ignition.

Regardless of your project plans, make sure to use all the required parts and follow the installation methods specified by the manufacturer and local building codes.

Planning the Project

NOTE: Consult the manufacturer's instructions for the specifications regarding placement, clearances, and venting methods for your fireplace.

Start your planning by determining the best location for the fireplace. Placing the unit next to an exterior wall simplifies the venting required. One important specification for a basement fireplace is that the termination cap (on the outside end of the vent) must be 12" above the ground. In the project shown, the vent runs upward 3 ft. before it turns at an elbow and passes through a masonry wall. Because the wall is non-combustible, no heat shield is needed around the vent penetration.

Next, design the frame. As long as it meets the clearance requirements for your fireplace, the frame can be any size and shape you like. Typical clearance minimums include a ½" space between the framing and the sides and back of the unit and a ¼" space above the standoffs (for positioning and adjusting the unit). The easiest way to build a frame is to use 2 × 4s and wallboard.

Finally, plan the rough-ins. Most fireplaces use a ½" gas supply line that connects directly to the unit. Check with the local gas utility or building department to determine what piping you'll need and the gas output required for your model. You may also need electrical wiring installed if your fireplace includes optional equipment, such as a blower or remote ignition. Complete the rough-ins after the frame is built. If you're not qualified to do the job yourself, hire professionals.

For help with any of these planning issues, talk with knowledgeable dealers in your area. They can help you choose the best fireplace model for your situation and assist you with venting and other considerations. And remember, all installation specifications are governed by local building codes. Check with the building department to make sure your plans conform to regulations.

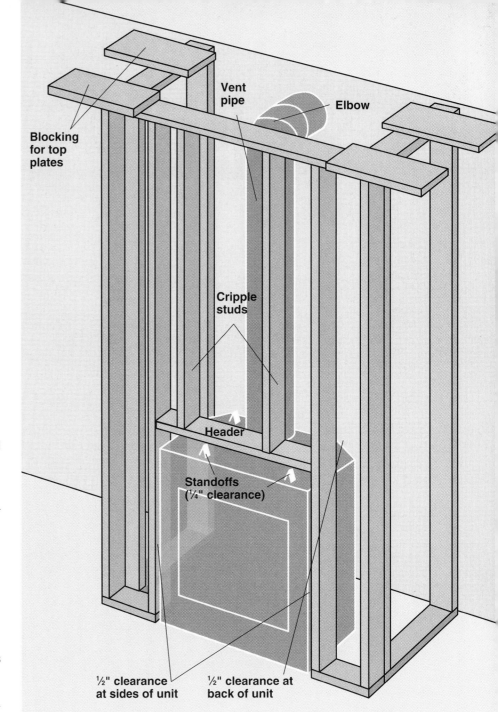

Blocking for top plates

Vent pipe

Elbow

Cripple studs

Header

Standoffs (¼" clearance)

½" clearance at sides of unit

½" clearance at back of unit

Everything You Need:

Tools: Framing square, chalk line, plumb bob, circular saw, drill, 2-ft. level, hammer drill, masonry bit, masonry chisel, hand maul, adjustable wrenches, brush, nail set, V-notched trowel, screwdriver, grout float, sponge.

Materials: Fireplace unit, vent sections, termination cap, ½" copper tubing, 2 × blocking lumber, 2 × 4 lumber, construction adhesive, masonry fasteners, 3" wallboard screws, sheet metal plates, plastic sheet, scrap plywood, sheet metal screws, caulk, ⅝" wallboard, wallboard finishing materials, high-temperature sealant, primer, paint, mantle, wood-finishing materials, 6d and 4d finish nails, wood putty, ceramic tile, tile spacers, latex tile adhesive, masking tape, grout, cap rail trim, buildup strips.

How to Install a Gas Fireplace

2 × blocking

Header

1 Mark the frame's outer edges onto the floor. Use a framing square to draw perpendicular lines for the side walls. Measure and mark the front of the frame with a chalk line. Measure diagonally from corner to corner to make sure the layout lines are square; adjust the lines, if necessary. Transfer the lines from the floor to the ceiling joists with a plumb bob. If any top plates fall between parallel joists, install 2 × blocking between the joists. Snap a line through the marks to complete the top-plate layout.

Cut the bottom plates to size from pressure-treated 2 × 4s. Position the plates inside the layout lines, and fasten them to the floor, using construction adhesive and masonry screws. (Option: use a powder-actuated nailer to fasten wood framing to masonry. Follow the tool manufacturer's instructions.) Cut the top plates from standard 2 × 4s, and attach them to the joists or blocking with 3" screws or 16d nails (drill pilot holes for screws). If the plates are attached directly to parallel joists, add backing for attaching the ceiling wallboard.

2 Mark the stud layout on the bottom plates, then transfer the layout to the top plates, using a plumb bob. Measure and cut the studs to length. Attach the two studs along the back wall using construction adhesive and masonry screws (or use a powder-actuated nailer). Attach the remaining studs to the top and bottom plates with 3" screws or 8d nails.

Measure up from the floor and mark the height of the header onto each stud at the side of the front opening. Cut and install the header. Cut the cripple studs to fit between the header and top plate. To allow easy access for running the vent pipe, do not install the cripple studs until after the vent is in place. Add any blocking needed to provide nailing surfaces for the ceramic tile trim.

(continued next page)

How to Install a Gas Fireplace (continued)

3 Bend out the nailing tabs at the sides of the fireplace unit. Slide the unit into the frame until the tabs meet the framing around the opening, then center the unit within the opening. Level the unit from side to side and front to back. Use thin sheet metal shims to make any adjustments. Apply a little construction adhesive to the shims to hold them in place. Measure at the sides and back of the unit to be sure the clearance requirements are met.

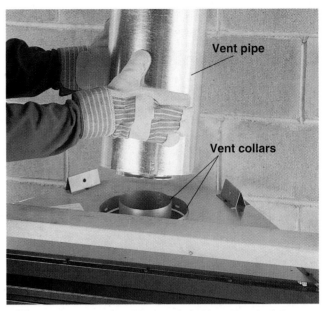

4 Dry-fit the vent pieces. Fit the flared end of the first vent section over the vent collars on top of the unit, aligning the inner and outer pipes of the vent with the matching collars. Push straight down on the vent until it snaps into place over the lugs on the outside of the collar. Pull up on the vent slightly to make sure it's locked into place.

5 Attach the 90° elbow so that the free end points toward the exterior wall. NOTE: Horizontal vent runs must slope upward ¼" per foot. If your vent includes additional horizontal sections leading from the elbow, adjust the vent pieces and elbow to follow the required slope. Trace the circumference of the elbow end onto the wall.

6 Remove the vent from the unit, and set it aside. Cover the fireplace with plastic and scrap plywood to protect it from debris. Using a long masonry bit and hammer drill, drill a series of holes just outside the marked circle, spacing them as close together as possible. Drill the holes all the way through the block. Be patient—the block cavities may be filled with concrete.

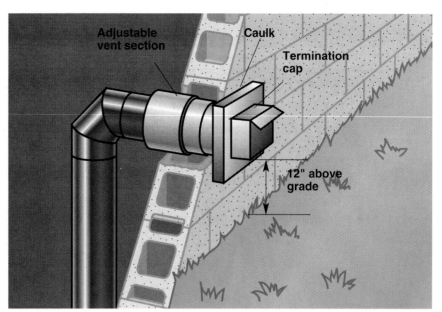

7 Carefully knock out the hole, using a masonry chisel and a hand maul. Work inward from both sides of the wall to ensure a clean cutout on the wall surfaces. Smooth the hole edges, test-fit the horizontal vent piece, and make any necessary adjustments. Uncover the fireplace, and clean up around the unit.

8 Reinstall the vertical vent section and elbow, locking the pieces together. Prepare the adjustable horizontal vent section by measuring the distance from the elbow to the termination cap. Adjust the section to length, and secure the sliding pieces together with two sheet metal screws. Install the horizontal vent section and termination cap, following the manufacturer's instructions. Seal around the cap perimeter with an approved caulk. When the vent run is complete, fasten the fireplace unit to the framing by driving screws through the nailing tabs. Install the cripple studs between the header and top plate.

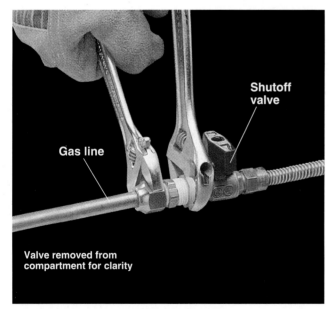

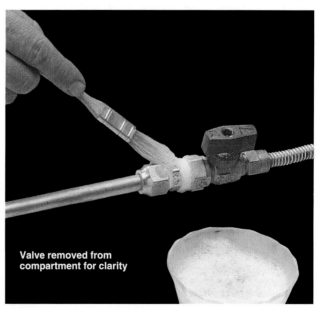

9 To make the gas connection, remove the lower grill from the front of the unit. Feed the gas supply pipe into the access hole on the side of the unit, and connect it to the manual shutoff valve. Tighten the connection with adjustable wrenches.

10 Turn on the gas supply, and check for leaks by brushing a solution of soapy water over the joint. If you see bubbles, you have a leak. Turn off the gas, tighten the connection, then retest it before proceeding.

(continued next page)

⅛" gaps

11 Before installing the wallboard, prepare the fire-box, and light the fire, following the manufacturer's instructions. Let the fire run for 15-20 minutes while you inspect the flame and vent. Report any problems to the manufacturer. Turn off the fireplace and let it cool down completely. Install ⅝" wallboard over the framing, running the panels horizontally and attaching them with screws. To provide space for sealant, leave a ⅛" gap between the wallboard and the top and sides of the front face of the unit.

12 Fill the gap around the front face with a high-temperature sealant supplied (or recommended) by the manufacturer. Tape and finish the wallboard seams (see page 115) and inside corner joints, and install and finish corner bead at the outside corners.

Mantle support cleat

13 To install the mantle, measure up from the floor and mark the height of the support cleat. Use a level to draw a level line through the mark. Mark the stud locations just above the level line. Position the cleat on the line, centered between the frame sides, and drill a pilot hole at each stud location. Fasten the cleat to the studs with screws provided by the manufacturer.

14 Prime and paint the areas of wallboard that won't be covered with tile. Finish the mantle as desired, then fit it over the support cleat and center it between the frame sides. Drill pilot holes for 6d finish nails through the top of the mantle, about ¾" from the back edge. Secure the mantle to the cleat with four nails. Set the nails with a nail set, fill the holes with wood putty, then touch up the finish.

15 Dry-fit the tile around the front of the fireplace. You can lay tile over the black front face, but do not cover the glass or any portion of the grills. If you're using floor tile without spacer lugs on the side edges, use plastic tile spacers to set the grout gaps between tiles (at least ⅛" for floor tile). Mark the perimeter of the tile area and make any other layout marks that will help with the installation. If possible, pre-cut any tiles.

16 Mask off around the tile, then use a V-notched trowel to apply latex mastic tile adhesive to the wall, spreading it evenly just inside the perimeter lines. Set the tiles into the adhesive, aligning them with the layout marks, and press firmly to create a good bond. Install spacers between tiles as you work, and scrape out excess adhesive from the grout joints, using a small screwdriver. Install all of the tile, then let the adhesive dry completely.

17 Mix a batch of grout, following the manufacturer's instructions. Spread the grout over the tiles with a rubber grout float, forcing the grout into the joints. Then, drag the float across the joints diagonally, tilting the float at an almost 90° angle. Make another diagonal pass to remove excess grout. Wait 10-15 minutes, then wipe smeared grout from the tile with a damp sponge, rinsing frequently. Let the grout dry for one hour, then polish the tiles with a dry cloth. Let the grout dry completely.

Cap rail trim

Buildup strip

18 Cut pieces of cap rail trim to fit around the tile, mitering the ends. If the tile is thicker than the trim recesses, install buildup strips behind the trim, using finish nails. Finish the trim to match the mantle. Drill pilot holes and nail the trim in place with 4d finish nails. Set the nails with a nail set. Fill the holes with wood putty and touch up the finish.

Storage & Shelving

Constructing Built-in Shelving

Permanent shelves can be built into any space around your home where storage is needed. The space between a door or window and an adjacent wall corner is often used for built-in shelving.

A shelving unit can be built out of any 1 × lumber except particleboard, which sags under heavy weight. For heavy loads, like books, a shelving unit should be built from 1 × 10 or 1 × 12 hardwood boards and should span no more than 48". Shelves can be supported from the ends by pegs or end clips.

When framing the basic shelving unit, build it 1" shorter than the floor to ceiling measurement . This allows you to tilt the unit into position without damaging the ceiling. Use trim moldings to hide gaps along the ceiling and floor.

Everything You Need

Tools: Tape measure, saw, framing square, scrap pegboard, drill and ¼" bit, hammer, nail set.

Materials: 1 × 10 or 1 × 12 hardwood lumber, 2 × 2 lumber, paint or wood stain, 6d finish nails, 12d common nails, trim molding, shelving pegs or end clips.

How to Construct a Built-in Shelving Unit

1 Measure the height and width of the available space. For easy installation, the basic unit is built 1" shorter than ceiling height. Remove the baseboards, and cut them to fit around the shelving unit. Replace the baseboards after the unit is nailed in place.

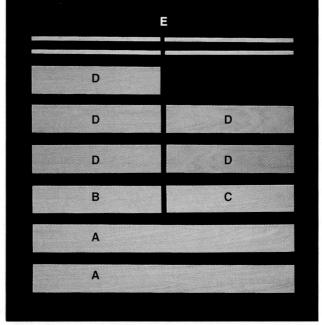

2 Mark and cut: two sides (A), 1" shorter than the floor to ceiling measurement; unit top (B), bottom (C), and shelves (D), each 1½" shorter than the unit width measurement; and four 2 × 2 frame supports (E),1½" shorter than the unit width measurement.

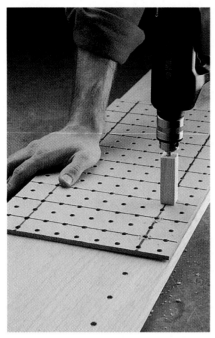

3 Using scrap pegboard as a guide, drill pairs of ¼" holes along the inside of each side (A), spaced horizontally 9" apart and vertically every 2". Holes should be ⅜" deep. Use scrap wood or a bit attachment as a depth guide.

4 Paint or stain the wood as desired before assembling the unit. Attach the sides (A) to the ends of the frame supports (E). Drill pilot holes and drive 6d finish nails through the sides and into the end grain of the frame supports.

5 Tilt the unit into position flush against the wall. Nail through the top rear frame support (E) into the wall studs, and through the bottom frame supports into the floor, using 12d common nails. Replace cut baseboards around the bottom of the shelving unit.

6 Attach the bottom (C) and top (B) inside the shelving unit. Drill pilot holes and drive 6d finish nails through the sides (A) into the end grain of the top and bottom.

7 Miter-cut trim molding to fit around the top and bottom of the shelving unit (see pages 20-23). Attach the trim with 6d finish nails. Use a nail set to recess all nail heads. Install shelving pegs or end clips in desired positions, then install shelves.

Building Glide-out Shelves

Base cabinets are the foundation for storage in many rooms in your home, and equipping them with these easy-to-build glide-out shelves will make them much more efficient. Glide-out shelves are an obvious choice for kitchen cabinets, but are equally useful wherever you have cabinet storage, including the pantry, laundry room, utility room, and recreation areas. In family rooms with cabinets, glide-out shelves provide a perfect place to store videos, family games and children's toys.

Installing glide-out shelves is quite easy, but you'll need to adapt the designs to accommodate face frames or concealed hinges that extend into the interior of the cabinet. You'll need to carefully measure the interior dimensions of the cabinets, calculate the reduction in space caused by face frames or hinges, and install spacer strips to make up this difference when mounting the glide-out tracks. The frameless cabinet shown in our project has fully concealed hinges that extend inward by about ¾", so we first installed ¾" spacer strips that would allow the shelves to move freely without hitting the hinges.

Everything You Need:

Tools: Jig saw, router with ½" straight bit and ¾" rabbet bit, hammer, clamps, drill with bits, nail set, circular saw, finishing sander.

Materials: (2) drawer glides, 4d finish nails, 1¼" utility screws, 120-grit sandpaper, 180-grit sandpaper, sanding sealer.

Key	Part	Dimension
A	(1) Shelf front	¾ × 3 × 26" hardwood
B	(1) Shelf back	¾ × 3 × 26" hardwood
C	(2) Shelf side	¾ × 3 × 22¼" hardwood
D	(1) Shelf bottom	½ × 25¼ × 22¼" plywood
E	(2) Spacer	¾ × 3 × 22¼" hardwood

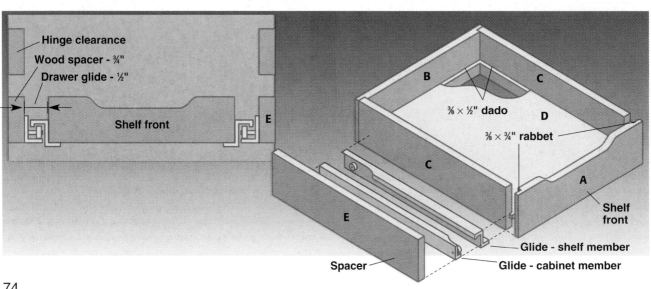

Hinge clearance
Wood spacer - ¾"
Drawer glide - ½"
Shelf front
E
B
C
⅜ × ½" dado
D
⅜ × ¾" rabbet
A
Shelf front
C
E
Spacer
Glide - shelf member
Glide - cabinet member

How to Build Glide-out Shelves

Step A: Cut the Shelf Pieces & Rout the Joints

1. Determine the size of the glide-out shelves by measuring the inside dimensions of the cabinet and subtracting the distance any objects protrude into the interior of the cabinet (hinges and face frames). Then subtract 1" from the width for the two slides and tracks (½" each).

2. Cut the front (A) and back (B) pieces for each shelf to the determined width. Then use a jig saw to cut out the top edge of the front pieces, making a decorative drawer pull area.

3. Determine the depth of the shelves by measuring the depth of the cabinet and subtracting 1". Cut the side pieces (C) for the shelves at this length.

4. Determine the width of the spacers (E), if they are necessary, and cut them to length to fit along the interior walls of the cabinet.

5. Cut the bottom pieces (D) to size from ½" plywood.

6. Install a ½" straight bit into the router and set the blade depth for ⅜". Cut a ⅜"-deep × ½"-wide dado into the front, back, and side panels, ½" from the bottom edges.

7. Install a ¾" rabbet bit into the router. Cut a ⅜"-deep × ¾"-wide rabbet groove on each end of the front and back pieces. Make sure the cuts fall on the inside faces of each piece.

Step B: Assemble the Shelves

1. Spread glue onto the rabbets of the shelf fronts and attach the sides, using three 4d finishing nails to hold each joint. Countersink the nails with a nail set.

2. Slide the bottom panels into the dado grooves. Then, glue and nail the back pieces in place. Clamp the shelves square, letting the glue dry.

3. Smooth all surfaces with a finishing sander and 120-grit sandpaper. Wipe off all dust, and coat the shelf with sanding sealer.

4. After the sealer has dried for an hour, lightly sand the shelves with 180-grit sandpaper. Apply a second coat of sealer.

Step C: Mount the Drawer Glides

1. Mount the cabinet halves of the drawer glides flush with the bottom edges of the spacer strips (E). Then attach the spacers to the interior walls of the cabinet with 1¼" utility screws. Use a level to ensure the glides are installed properly.

2. Screw the other half of each drawer glide to the sides of the shelves. Make sure the bottom edges of the glides are flush against the bottom shelf edges.

3. Install each shelf by aligning the drawer glides and pushing it completely in. The tracks will automatically lock into place.

A Rout dado and rabbet grooves in the 1 × 3.

B Apply glue to the rabbet joints and nail the front pieces of the shelves to the sides.

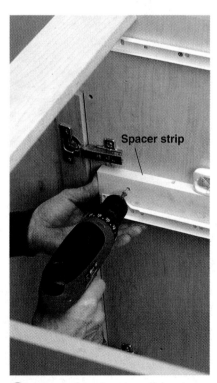

Spacer strip

C Attach the drawer glides to the spacer strips and attach the strips to the interior of the cabinet.

Building Recessed Wall Shelves

Turn the unused space inside your walls into custom-made, built-in storage. This project's narrow shelving could be used as a decorative display unit in the living room or an easy-access spice rack in the kitchen; the possible uses are limited only by your creativity. These easy-to-build, recessed shelves can be installed in any non-load-bearing interior wall, except in areas where electrical wires or plumbing pipes are located.

The project as shown is 30" wide—the width of two stud cavities spaced 16" on center. To duplicate these shelves, you will need to cut away one wall stud and install a sill and header. Never cut away more than one stud when building recessed shelving. You may, however, build a narrower cabinet by building the shelves into a single stud cavity between adjacent studs.

Everything You Need

Tools: Pencil, level, jig saw, reciprocating saw, power screwdriver, drill, right-angle drill guide, pegboard scraps, pipe clamps, hammer, tape measure, utility knife.

Materials: Wood glue, 8d and 10d finish nails, 1¾" and 2½" wood screws, 1" wire nails, pin-style shelf supports, wood shims.

Ideas for Recessed Shelving

Adapt recessed shelving to create a small game or storage cabinet by adding doors.

Create a pass-through between rooms by opening the wall from both sides and installing a wide shelf.

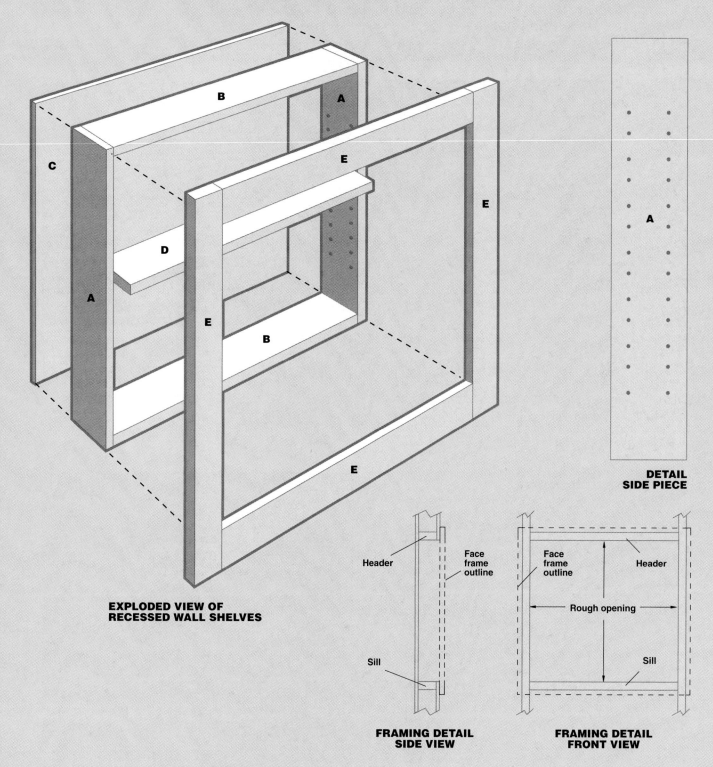

DETAIL SIDE PIECE

EXPLODED VIEW OF RECESSED WALL SHELVES

FRAMING DETAIL SIDE VIEW

Header

Face frame outline

Sill

FRAMING DETAIL FRONT VIEW

Face frame outline

Header

Rough opening

Sill

Parts List: Recessed Wall Shelves

	Project as Shown				Your Project	
Key	**Piece**	**Material**	**Pieces**	**Size**	**Pieces**	**Size**
A	Sides	1 × 4 oak	2	30"		
B	Top & bottom	1 × 4 oak	2	28³/₄"		
C	Back panel	³/₄" oak plywood	1	30" × 29¹/₂"		
D	Shelves	1 × 4 oak	3	28⁵/₈"		
E	Face frame	1 × 4 oak	11 linear ft.			
F	Header and sill plates	2 × 4	2	30¹/₂"		

How to Build Recessed Shelving

1 Locate the wall studs in the area where the shelves will be installed. Mark the cutout on the wall, using a level as a guide. The sides of the cutout should follow the edges of the wall studs and the height of the cutout should allow for the thickness of a header and sill. Make the cutout with a jig saw. CAUTION: Check for plumbing and electrical cables and make sure the wall is non-load-bearing before cutting.

2 Cut away the center stud at the top and bottom edge of the opening, using a reciprocating saw. Use a flat pry bar to remove the cut portion of the stud. (You may need to patch the opposite wall surface if it is screwed or nailed to the stud you remove.)

3 Measure between the side studs at the top and bottom edges of the opening, and cut header and sill to fit. Attach the header and sill to the cripple studs and side studs with 3" screws. Remeasure the height of the opening between the header and sill.

4 Cut side pieces ¼" shorter than the measured height of the opening. Cut top and bottom pieces 1¾" shorter than the measured width. Drill two rows of holes on the inside face of each side piece to hold pin-style shelf supports. Use a scrap piece of pegboard as a template and a right-angle drill guide to ensure that the holes on facing pieces will be lined up properly.

5 Glue and clamp the side pieces around the top and bottom pieces to form butt joints. Use a square to make sure the frame is square. Drill counterbored pilot holes into the joints, and reinforce them with 1¾" wood screws.

6 Measure and cut a ¼" plywood back panel to fit flush with the outside edges of the frame. Attach the back with 1" wire nails driven every 4" to 5". To allow for natural expansion and contraction, do not glue the back panel.

7 Position the box in the opening and shim until it is level and plumb and the front edges are flush with the wall surface. Drill pilot holes, and anchor the cabinet to the side studs, header and sill, using 8d finish nails driven every 6" to 8" and through the shim locations. Trim the shims with a utility knife.

8 Measure the inside height and width of the cabinet box, then cut 1 × 4 horizontal face frame rails equal to the width, and 1 × 4 vertical stiles 7" longer than the height. Glue and clamp the rails between the stiles to form butt joints. Reinforce the joints by drilling angled pilot holes and toenailing 10d finish nails through the stiles and into the rails.

9 Position the face frame, drill pilot holes, and attach with 8d finish nails driven into the top, bottom, and side panels, and into the framing members. Countersink nails, fill nail holes, sand, and finish the project. Build and install adjustable shelves ⅛" shorter than the distance between side panels.

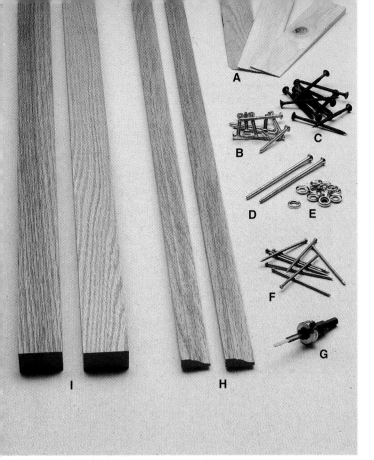

Specialty tools & supplies include: wood shims (A), No. 8-gauge 2½" sheetmetal screws (B), 3" wallboard screws (C), No. 10-gauge 4" wood screws (D), finish washers (E), 6d finish nails (F), No. 9 counterbore drill bit (G), trim moldings (H), filler strips (I).

Adding New Cabinets

Stock base cabinets and wall cabinets can be a good addition to many spaces in your home—not just the kitchen and bathroom. Organized storage improves almost any room. The recreation room, laundry, workshop, nursery, or garage all benefit from well chosen and properly installed cabinets.

Installing cabinets is fairly simple; with one or two helpers, most people can do a fine job of installing them. If you are planning to replace the flooring, or make electrical or plumbing changes in the area, finish the work before beginning the installation of cabinets.

Preparing the walls for new cabinetry is one of the most important steps of cabinet installation. Walls that are not flat and plumb will make the installation difficult and affect the overall appearance of the cabinets once the installation is complete. Make sure that you take the time to identify any high and low spots on the walls, and install the temporary ledger as level as possible.

Cabinets should be firmly anchored to wall studs, and must be exactly plumb and level so that the doors and drawers operate smoothly. Number each cabinet and mark its position on the wall. Remove the cabinet doors and drawers, and number them so they can be easily replaced after the cabinets are installed.

Before you begin screwing cabinets to the wall, make sure the electricity to the area is off. If you are installing both base and wall cabinets, begin with the wall cabinets. Where cabinets run along two walls, start at a corner, otherwise begin at either end. Correct placement of the corner cabinets is essential to making the adjacent cabinets plumb.

Before installation, test-fit corner and adjoining cabinets to make sure doors and handles do not interfere with each other. If necessary, increase the clearance by pulling the blind cabinet away from side wall by no more than 4" (C). To maintain even spacing between the edges of doors and cabinet corner (A, B), cut a filler strip and attach it to the adjoining cabinet. Measure distance (C) as a reference when positioning the blind cabinet against the wall.

Everything You Need:

Tools: Tape measure, pencil, stud finder, trowel, sandpaper, handscrew clamps, level, hammer, utility knife, nail set, stepladder, drill with ³/₁₆" twist bit and counterbore bit, cordless screwdriver, jig saw with wood-cutting blade.

Materials: 1 × 3 dimensional lumber, a straight 2 × 4, wallboard compound, 2½" wallboard screws, cabinets, 2½" sheetmetal screws, toe-kick molding, valance, wood putty, cleats, specialty supplies (photo, above left).

How to Prepare Walls for New Cabinets

1 Find the high and low spots on the wall surfaces, using a long, straight 2 × 4. Sand down any high spots.

2 Fill in any low spots of the wall. Apply wallboard taping compound with a trowel, and sand it lightly after the compound dries.

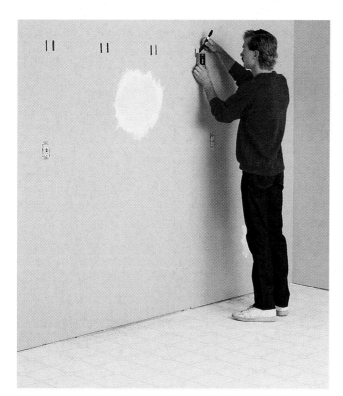

3 Locate and mark all wall studs in the project area, using an electronic stud finder. The cabinets will be hung by driving screws into the studs through the back of the cabinets.

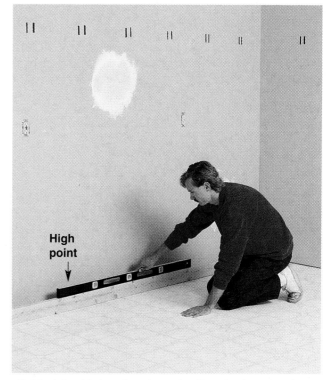

High point

4 Find the high point along the floor in the area that will be covered by the base cabinets. Place a level on a long, straight 2 × 4, and move the board along the floor to determine if the floor is uneven. If so, mark the wall at the high point.

(continued next page)

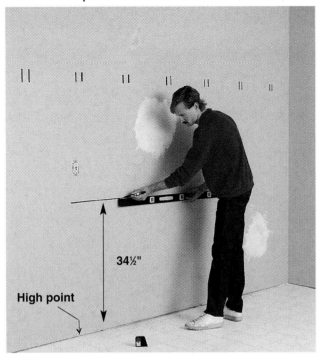

5 Measure up 34½" from the high-point mark. Use a level to mark a reference line on the walls. The base cabinets will be installed with the top edges flush against this line.

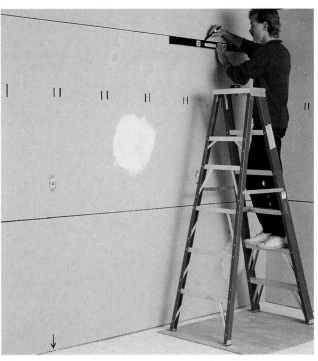

6 Measure up 84" from the high-point mark and draw a second reference line. When installed, the top edges of the wall cabinets will be flush on this line.

7 Measure down 30" from the wall-cabinet reference line and draw another level line where the bottom of cabinets will be. Temporary ledgers will be installed against this line.

8 Install 1 × 3 temporary ledgers with the top edge flush against the reference line. Attach the ledgers with 2½" wallboard screws driven into every other stud. Mark the stud locations on the ledgers. The cabinets will rest on the ledgers during installation.

How to Install Wall Cabinets

1 Position the corner cabinet on the ledger. Drill ¾₆" pilot holes into studs through the hanging strips at rear of cabinet. Attach the cabinet to the wall with 2½" sheetmetal screws. Do not tighten fully until all cabinets are hung.

2 Attach filler strip to adjoining cabinet, if needed (see page 80). Clamp the filler in place, and drill pilot holes through the cabinet face frame near the hinge locations, using a counterbore bit. Attach the filler to the cabinet with 2½" sheetmetal screws.

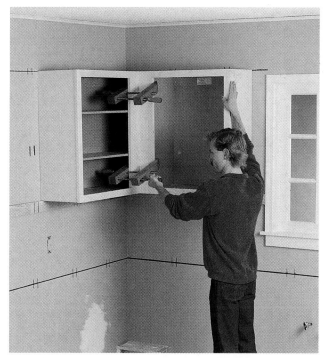

3 Position the adjoining cabinet on the ledger, tight against the blind corner cabinet. Check the face frame for plumb. Drill ¾₆" pilot holes into the wall studs through the hanging strips in rear of cabinet. Attach the cabinet with 2½" sheetmetal screws. Do not tighten wall screws fully until all cabinets are hung.

4 Clamp the corner cabinet and the adjoining cabinet together at the top and bottom of the cabinets. NOTE: Handscrew clamps will not damage the wood face frames.

(continued next page)

5 Attach the blind corner cabinet to the adjoining cabinet from inside the corner cabinet. Drill pilot holes through the face frames and join the cabinets with sheetmetal screws.

6 Position and attach each additional cabinet. Clamp the frames together, and drill counterbored pilot holes through the sides of the face frames. Join the cabinets with sheetmetal screws. Drill ³⁄₁₆" pilot holes in the hanging strips, and anchor the cabinets to the studs with sheetmetal screws.

Variation: Join frameless cabinets with No. 8-gauge 1¼" wood screws and finish washers. Each pair of cabinets should be joined by at least four screws.

7 Fill small spaces between a cabinet and a wall or appliance with a filler strip. Cut the strip to fit the space and wedge it into place with wood shims. Drill counterbored pilot holes through the side of the cabinet face frame. Attach filler with sheetmetal screws.

8 Remove the temporary ledger. Check the cabinet run for plumb, and adjust it if necessary by placing wood shims behind the cabinet, near the stud locations. Tighten the wall screws completely. Cut off the shims with a utility knife.

9 Use trim moldings to cover any gaps between the cabinets and walls. Stain or paint the moldings to match the cabinet finish and attach them to the cabinet sides with finish nails.

10 Install the cabinet doors following the cabinet manufacturer's instructions. If necessary, adjust the hinges so that the doors are straight and plumb.

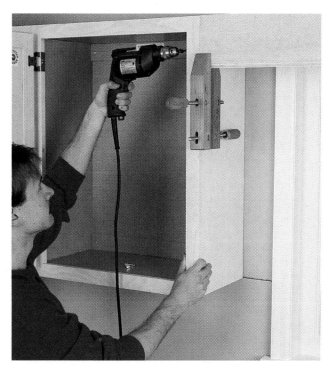

Variation: Attach a decorative valence above a sink to hide future utility lighting. Clamp the valence to the edge of the cabinet frames, and drill counterbored pilot holes through the cabinet frames into the end of the valence. Attach it with sheetmetal screws.

How to Install Base Cabinets

1 Begin the installation with a corner cabinet. Position the cabinet so that the top is flush with the reference line (see page 82). Make sure the cabinet is plumb and level. If necessary, adjust the cabinet by driving wood shims under the base. (Be careful not to damage the flooring.) Drill ³⁄₁₆" pilot holes through the cabinet hanging strip into the wall studs. Attach the cabinets loosely to the wall with 2½" sheetmetal screws.

2 Attach a filler strip to the adjoining cabinet, if necessary (see pages 80 and 83). Clamp the filler in place, and drill counterbored pilot holes through the side of the face frame. Attach the filler with sheetmetal screws.

3 Clamp the adjoining cabinet to the corner cabinet. Make sure the cabinet is plumb, then drill counterbored pilot holes through the corner-cabinet face frame into the filler strip (see page 84, step 5). Join the cabinets with sheetmetal screws. Drill ³⁄₁₆" pilot holes through the hanging strip into the wall studs. Attach the cabinets loosely with sheetmetal screws.

4 Use a jig saw to cut any openings needed for plumbing, wiring, or heating ducts.

5 Position and attach any additional cabinets, making sure the frames are aligned. Clamp the cabinets together, then drill counterbored pilot holes through the sides of the face frames. Join the cabinets with sheetmetal screws. Frameless cabinets are joined with No. 8-gauge 1¼" wood screws and finish washers (see variation, page 84).

6 Make sure all the cabinets are level. If necessary, adjust by driving wood shims underneath the cabinets. Place wood shims behind the cabinets near stud locations wherever there is a gap. Tighten the wall screws. Cut off the shims with a utility knife.

7 Use trim moldings to cover any gaps between the cabinets and the wall or floor. The toe-kick area is often covered with a strip of hardwood finished to match the cabinets.

8 If the corner has a void area not covered by cabinets, screw 1 x 3 cleats to the wall, flush with the reference line. The cleats wil help support the countertop.

Doors & Windows

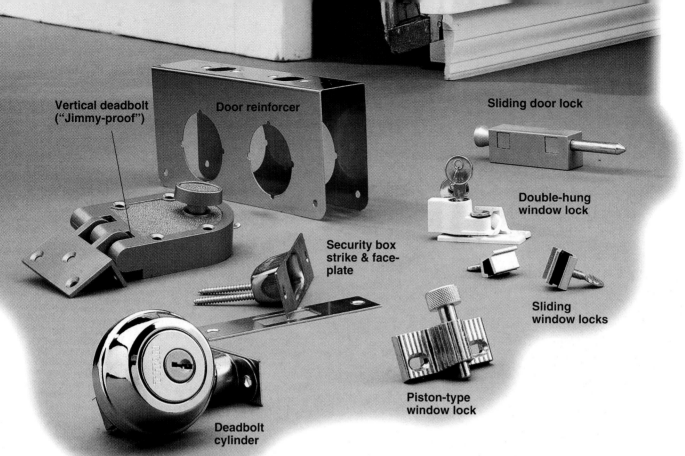

Vertical deadbolt ("Jimmy-proof")

Door reinforcer

Sliding door lock

Double-hung window lock

Security box strike & face-plate

Sliding window locks

Deadbolt cylinder

Piston-type window lock

Securing Doors & Windows

Keeping your home secure from intruders is critical to your comfort level and quality of life. Securing doors and windows is simply a matter of having the right hardware. There are four basic elements in door security: the door, the lock, the frame, and the hinges. Skimping on strength or quality with any one of these will undermine the security of the whole system.

Entry doors should be metal or solid wood—at least 1¾" thick—and each one in the house should have a dead-bolt lock, as doorknob locks provide little security.

A lock is only as good as its mounting hardware: Use long, sturdy screws for mounting locks to doors. Another important piece of hardware is the *strike plate*—the flat metal plate that receives the lock bolt. Standard strike plates are screwed into the door frame alone and may be backed by less than ½" of wood. For more strength, install a *security box strike*. This device has a deep metal pocket for supporting the bolt and includes long mounting screws that reach well into the wall studs.

Door hinges are easy to secure. You can add plenty of strength by replacing two screws on each hinge with longer screws that penetrate wall studs. If the hinge pins are on the outside of the door, install a set of *hinge enforcers*. These inexpensive devices hold a door in place even when the hinge pins are removed.

Door frames are susceptible to being pried outward, which frees the lock bolt. To defend against this kind of attack, stiffen the door frame by adding plywood shims between the frame and wall studs.

Garage doors are structurally secure, but their locking devices can make them easy targets. When you're away from home, place a padlock in the roller track. If you have an automatic door opener, make sure the remote transmitter uses a rolling code system, which prevents thieves from copying your signal. An electronic keypad can make your garage door as secure and easy to use as your front door.

Glass is both the strength and weakness of windows, in terms of security. An intruder can easily break the glass, but the noise it makes is likely to draw attention. Aside from installing metal bars, there's no way to secure the glass, so make sure your windows can't be opened from the outside. There's a host of inexpensive locks available for every type of window.

You can also secure windows using simple hardware items, such as screws and dowels. And when it comes to securing sliding glass doors, think of them as a big windows: Add extra locks and install screws to prevent the panels from being pried from their tracks.

Everything You Need

Tools: Drill, screwdriver, saw.

Materials: (as needed) Screws, board, hinge, eyebolts, dowel, security devices.

Tips for Securing Doors

Add metal door reinforcers to strengthen the areas around locks and prevent kick-ins. Remove the lockset and slip the reinforcer over the door's edge. Be sure to get a reinforcer that is the correct thickness for your door.

Add a heavy-duty latch guard to reinforce the door jamb around the strike plate. For added protection, choose a guard with a flange that resists pry-bar attacks. Install the guard with long screws that reach the wall studs.

Replace short hinge screws with longer screws (3" or 4") that extend through the door jamb and into the wall studs. This helps resist door kick-ins. Tighten the screws until snug, but avoid over-tightening them, which can pull the frame out of square.

Tips for Securing Sliding Glass Doors

Make a custom lock for your door track, using a thick board and a hinge. Cut the board to fit behind the closed door, then cut it again a few inches from one end. Install a hinge and knob so you can flip up the end and keep the door secure while it's ajar.

Drive screws partially into the upper track to keep the sliding panel from being pried up and out of the lower track. Use sturdy panhead screws, spaced about every 8", and drive them so their heads just clear the top of the door. For metal door frames, use self-tapping screws and a low drill speed.

Attach a deadbolt lock to the frame of the sliding panel. Drill a hole for the deadbolt into the upper track. Then, drill an additional hole a few inches away so you can lock the door in an open position.

Tips for Securing Windows

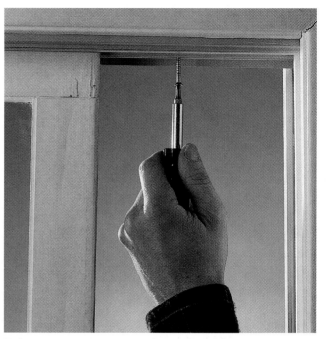

Pin together sashes of single- and double-hung windows with ¼" × 3" eye bolts. With the window closed, drill a ¼"-dia. hole, at a slight downward angle, through the top rail of the bottom sash and into the bottom rail of the top sash. Stop the hole about ¾ of the way through the top sash. To lock the window in open positions, drill holes along the sash stiles (vertical pieces) instead.

Drive screws into the top channel of sliding windows to prevent intruders from lifting the window sash out of the lower channel. The screws should just clear the top of the window and not interfere with its operation. Use sturdy screws, and space them about 6" apart.

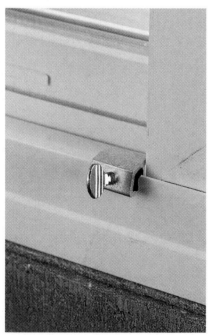

Block sash channels on sliding windows with a narrow board or a thick dowel.

Use auxiliary locks on sliding windows when a dowel or board won't work. Most types can be installed on the upper or lower window track.

Replace old sash locks on double-hung windows with keyed devices. Traditional sash locks can be highly vulnerable—especially on old windows. Be sure to store a key nearby, for emergency escape.

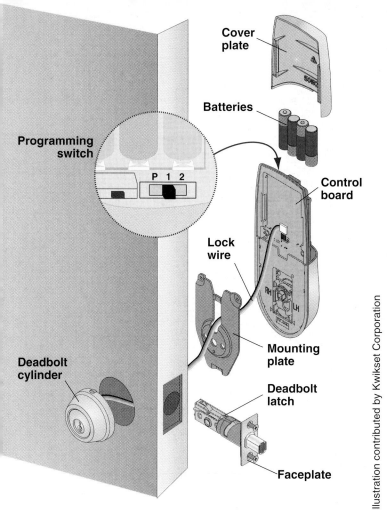

Cover plate

Batteries

Programming switch

P 1 2

Control board

Lock wire

Mounting plate

Deadbolt latch

Deadbolt cylinder

Faceplate

Illustration contributed by Kwikset Corporation

Installing a Keyless Entry Deadbolt

Keyless entry provides home security with the push of a button. These systems generally work with either a small keychain remote or a programmable keypad. It is a great addition if you have children who must come home to an empty house after school. After you teach your children the keypad code, you won't have to worry about lost or stolen keys.

If you are replacing an old deadbolt with a keyless entry system, don't assume that the new lock will fit the existing holes. If the door and jamb holes are slightly misaligned the lock will not work properly. Consult the manufacturer's directions for measurement requirements, and make sure the holes in the door and jamb are properly sized and aligned.

Everything You Need

Tools: Awl, drill with ⅛" bit, hole saw, spade bits, utility knife, hammer, chisel, flathead and Phillips screwdrivers.

Materials: Keyless entry deadbolt kit, nail, 3" wood screws.

How to Install a Keyless Entry Deadbolt

1 Tape the template supplied with your lock to the door in the desired location, usually about 5½" above the existing lockset. Mark the center positions for the cylinder and deadbolt holes with an awl (inset). Then, drill pilot holes at the marked points entirely through the door face and 2" deep into the door edge.

2 Use a drill and hole saw of the recommended size to bore the cylinder hole. To avoid splintering the wood, drill through one side until the pilot bit comes through, then finish drilling the hole from the other side.

(continued next page)

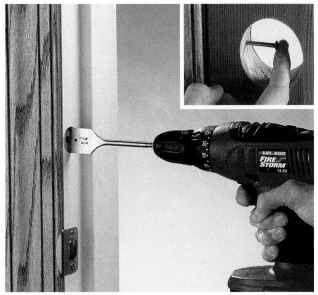

3 Mark the center of the strike box onto the door-jamb by closing the door and pressing a nail from inside the cylinder hole through the pilot hole in the door edge until it marks the door jamb (inset). Use the recommended spade bit to bore a 1"-deep hole into the jamb. Bore the deadbolt latch hole through the door edge and into the cylinder hole, using the recommended spade bit.

4 Insert the deadbolt latch into the edge hole and hold it in place temporarily with the included screws. Score around the faceplate with a utility knife (inset). Then, remove the latch and use a hammer and chisel to carefully remove material until the faceplate fits flush with the door. Attach the faceplate to the door with the included screws.

5 Insert the strike box into the door jamb, and make sure the deadbolt is precisely aligned with the strike plate. Mark and chisel out a recess so the strike plate is flush with the jamb. Drill pilot holes and install the strike plate with 3" wood screws.

6 Fit the exterior portion of the lock into the cylinder hole, sliding the cylinder tailpiece through the proper hole on the deadbolt. Route the lock wire underneath the deadbolt, making sure it is free of any moving parts. Fit the wire through the proper hole on the interior mounting plate and attach the plate to the deadbolt with the included screws.

7 Follow the manufacturer's instructions to align your lock control for a left- or right-hand door. Plug the lock wire into the receiving wire on the interior control board. With the bolt extended and the knob in the vertical position, slide the board into place and attach it with the included screws. Install the batteries and follow the manufacturer's instructions to program the remote and entry codes.

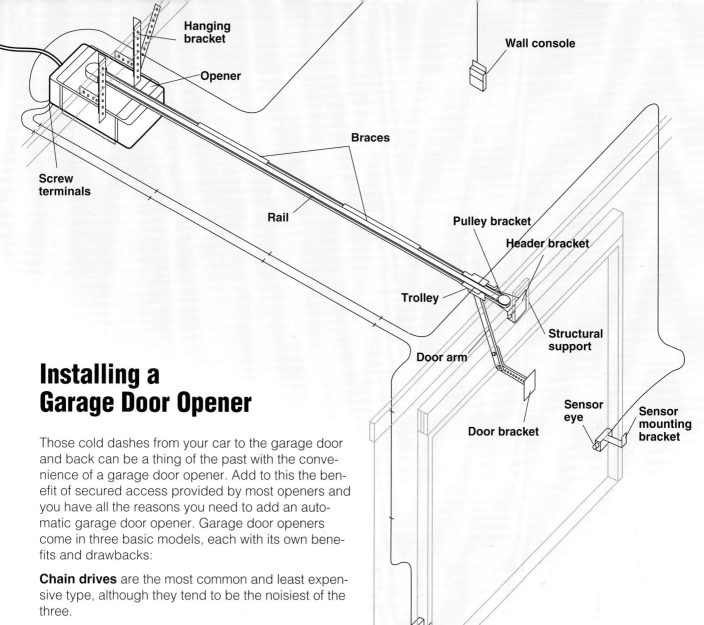

Hanging bracket

Opener

Screw terminals

Wall console

Braces

Rail

Pulley bracket

Header bracket

Trolley

Structural support

Door arm

Sensor eye

Door bracket

Sensor mounting bracket

Installing a Garage Door Opener

Those cold dashes from your car to the garage door and back can be a thing of the past with the convenience of a garage door opener. Add to this the benefit of secured access provided by most openers and you have all the reasons you need to add an automatic garage door opener. Garage door openers come in three basic models, each with its own benefits and drawbacks:

Chain drives are the most common and least expensive type, although they tend to be the noisiest of the three.

Belt drives run on a fiber-reinforced rubber belt. They are the quietest but also the most expensive. Consider a belt drive if your garage is below or adjacent to a living area.

Screw drive systems employ a long, threaded rod to open the door and are quiet and relatively maintenance-free. They are usually priced between the chain and belt drive types. The slow opening speed of most screw drives makes them ideal for one-piece doors, which run more smoothly when opened slowly.

This project shows the basic steps for installing a chain drive system on a sectional door in a garage with exposed joists. If you have a one-piece door, a lightweight metal or glass panelled door, or a garage with a finished ceiling, consult the manufacturer's directions for alternative installation procedures.

Before you begin, make sure your garage door is properly balanced and moves smoothly. Open and close the door to see if it sticks or binds at any point. Release the door in the half-open position. It should

stay in place, supported by its own springs. If your door is not balanced or sticks at any point in its path, call a garage door service professional before attempting the opener installation.

Most garage door openers plug into a standard grounded receptacle located near the unit. Some local codes may require openers to be hard-wired into circuits. Consult the manufacturer's directions for hard-wiring procedures.

Everything You Need

Tools: Stepladder, tape measure, screwdriver, pliers, wire cutters, pencil, hammer, adjustable wrench, ½" and ⁷⁄₁₆" sockets and ratchet wrench, drill and bits.

Materials: Garage door opener kit, 2 × lumber (for door header, if necessary).

How to Install a Garage Door Opener

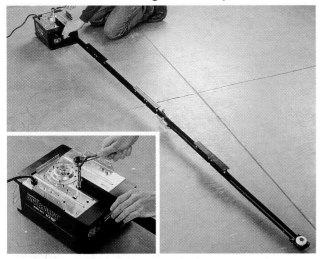

1 Start by aligning the rail pieces in proper order and securing them with the included braces and bolts. Screw the pulley bracket to the door-end of the rail and slide the trolley onto the rail. Make sure the pulley and all rail pieces are properly aligned and that the trolley runs smoothly without hitting any hardware along the rail. Remove the two screws from the top of the opener, then attach the rail to the opener using these screws (inset).

2 The drive chain/cable should be packaged in its own dispensing carton. Attach the cable loop to the front of the trolley using the included linking hardware. Wrap the cable around the pulley, then wrap the remaining chain around the drive sprocket on the opener. Finally, attach it to the other side of the trolley with linking hardware. Make sure the chain is not twisted, then attach the cover over the drive sprocket. Tighten the chain by adjusting the nuts on the trolley until the chain is ½" above the base of the rail.

3 To locate the header bracket, first extend a vertical line from the center of the door onto the wall above. Raise the door and note the highest point the door reaches. Measure from the floor to this point. Add 2" to this distance and mark a horizontal line on the front wall where it intersects the center line. If there is no structural support behind the cross point, fasten 2 × lumber across the framing. Then, fasten the header bracket to the structural support with the included screws.

4 Support the opener on the floor with a board or box to prevent stress and twisting to the rail. Attach the rail pulley bracket to the header bracket above the door with the included clevis pin. Then, place the opener on a stepladder so it is above the door tracks. Open the door and shim beneath the opener until the rail is 2" above the door.

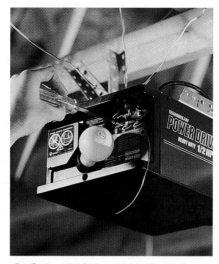
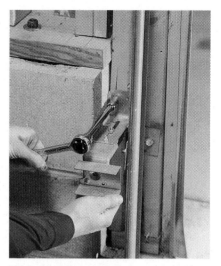

5 Hang the opener from the ceiling joists with the included hanging brackets and screws. Angle at least one of the hanging brackets to ensure stability. Attach the manual release cord and handle to the release arm of the trolley.

6 Strip ¼" of sheathing from the wall-console bell wire. Connect the wire to the screw terminals on the console, then attach it to the inside wall of the garage with included screws. Run the wires up the wall and connect them to the proper terminals on the opener. Secure the wire to the wall with insulated staples, being careful not to pierce the wire. Install the light bulbs and lenses.

7 Install the sensor eye mounting brackets at each side of the garage door, parallel to each other, about 4" to 6" from the floor. The sensor brackets can be attached to the door track, the wall, or the floor, depending upon your garage layout. See the manufacturer's directions for the best configuration for your garage.

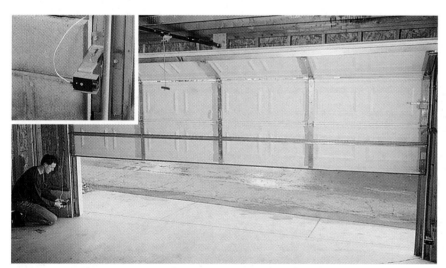

8 Attach the sensor eyes to the brackets with the included wing nuts, but do not tighten the nuts completely. Make sure the path of the eyes is unobstructed by the door tracks. Run wires from both sensors to the opener unit and connect the wires to the proper terminals. Plug the opener into a grounded receptacle and adjust the sensors until the indicator light shows correct eye alignment, then tighten the wing nuts. Unplug the unit and attach the sensor wires to the walls with insulated staples.

9 Center the door bracket 2" to 4" below the top of the door. Drill holes and attach the bracket with the included carriage bolts. Connect the straight and curved arm sections with the included bolts. Attach the arm to the trolley and door bracket with the included latch pins. Plug the opener into a grounded receptacle and test the unit. See the manufacturer's directions for adjustment procedures.

Installing a Storm Door

No matter your climate, a storm door can improve the appearance and weather resistance of an old entry door, or protect a newly installed door against weathering. Equipped with both glass and screen, storm doors allow control of both light and ventillation in your home, as well.

A popular style is the glass pane door, which allows a full view of your front door while still protecting it from the elements. For highly used entries, especially in homes with pets or children, storm doors with a solid lower half may be the best choice. Before you purchase a storm door, carefully note the dimensions of your door opening, measuring from the inside edges of the entry door's brick molding. Make sure to choose a storm door that opens from the same side as your entry door.

Everything You Need

Tools: Tape measure, pencil, plumb bob, hacksaw, hammer, drill and bits, screwdrivers.

Materials: Storm door unit, wood spacer strips, 4d casing nails.

How to Cut a Storm Door Frame to Fit a Door Opening

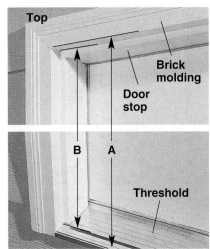

1 Because entry door thresholds are slanted, the bottom of the storm door frame needs to be cut to match the threshold angle. Measure from the threshold to the top of the door opening along the corner of the brick molding (A), then measure along the front edge of the entry door stop (B).

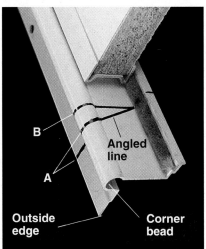

2 Subtract ⅛" from measurements A and B to allow for small adjustments when the door is installed. Measuring from the top of the storm door frame, mark the adjusted points A and B on the corner bead. Draw a line from point A to the outside edge of the frame and from point B to the inside edge. Draw an angled line from point A on the corner bead to point B on the inside edge.

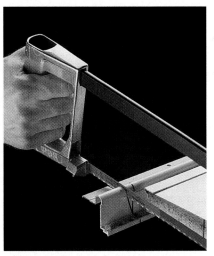

3 Use a hacksaw to cut down through the bottom of the storm door frame, following the angled line. Make sure to hold the hacksaw at the same slant as the angled line to ensure that the cut will be smooth and straight.

How to Fit & Install a Storm Door

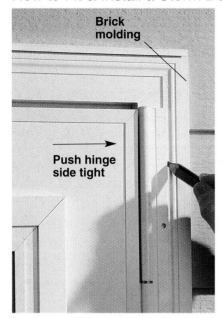

1 Position the storm door in the opening and push the frame tight against the brick molding on the hinge side of the storm door, then draw a reference line on the brick molding, following the edge of the storm door frame.

2 Push the storm door frame tight against the brick molding on the latch side, then measure the gap between the reference line and the hinge side of the door frame. If the distance is greater than ⅜", spacer strips must be installed to ensure the door will fit snugly.

3 To install spacers, remove the door then nail thin strips of wood to the inside of the brick molding at the storm door hinge locations. The thickness of the wood strips should be ⅛" less than the gap measured in step 2.

4 Replace the storm door and push it tight against the brick molding on the hinge side. Drill pilot holes through the hinge side frame of the storm door and into the brick molding spaced every 12". Attach the frame with mounting screws.

5 Remove any spacer clips holding the frame to the storm door. With the storm door closed, drill pilot holes and attach the latch side frame to the brick molding. Use a coin to keep an even gap between the storm door and the storm door frame.

6 Center the top piece of the storm door frame on top of the frame sides. Drill pilot holes and screw the top piece to the brick molding. Adjust the bottom sweep, then attach the locks and latch hardware as directed by the manufacturer.

Installing a Tubular Skylight

Any interior room can be brightened with a tubular skylight. Unlike traditional skylights, tubular skylights are quite energy efficient and are relatively easy to install, with no complicated framing involved.

Tubular skylights vary among manufacturers, with some using solid plastic reflecting tubes and others using flexible tubing. Various diameters are also available. Measure the distance between the framing members in your attic before purchasing your skylight.

This project shows the installation of a tubular skylight on a sloped, asphalt-shingled roof. Consult the dealer or manufacturer for installation procedures on other roof types.

Photo courtesy of Sun Tunnel Systems, Inc.

Everything You Need

Tools: Pencil, drill, tape measure, wallboard saw, reciprocating saw or jig saw, prybar, screwdriver, hammer, wire cutters, utility knife, chalk.

Materials: Tubular skylight kit, stiff wire, 2" roofing nails or flashing screws, roofing cement.

How to Install a Tubular Skylight

1 Drill a pilot hole through the ceiling at the approximate location for your skylight. Fish a stiff wire into the attic to help locate the hole. In the attic, make sure the space around the hole is clear and pull back any insulation. Drill a second hole through the ceiling at the centerpoint between two joists.

2 Center the ceiling ring frame over the hole and trace around it with a pencil. Carefully cut out along the pencil line with a wallboard saw or reciprocating saw. Save the wallboard ceiling cutout to use as your roof-hole pattern. Attach the ceiling frame ring around the hole with the included screws.

3 In the attic, choose the most direct route for the tubing to reach the roof. Find the center between the appropriate rafters and drive a nail up through the roof sheathing and shingles.

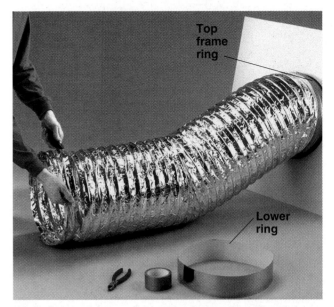

4 Use the wallboard ceiling cutout, centered over the nail hole, as a template for the roof opening. Trace the cutout onto the roof with chalk. Drill a starter hole to insert the reciprocating saw blade, then cut out the hole in the roof. Pry up the lower portion of the shingles above the hole. Remove any staples or nails around the hole edge.

5 Pull the tubing over the top frame ring. Bend the frame tabs out through the tubing, keeping two or three rings of the tubing wire above the tabs. Wrap the junction three times around with included PVC tape. Then, in the attic, measure from the roof to the ceiling. Stretch out the tubing and cut it to length with a utility knife and wire cutters. Pull the loose end of tubing over the lower ring and wrap it three times around with PVC tape.

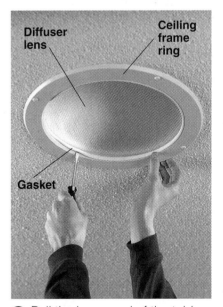

6 Lower the tubing through the roof hole and slide the flashing into place with the upper portion of the flashing underneath the existing shingles. This is easier with two people, one on the roof and one in the attic.

7 Secure the flashing to the roof with 2" roofing nails or flashing screws. Seal under the shingles and over all nail heads with roofing cement. Attach the skylight dome and venting to the frame with the included screws.

8 Pull the lower end of the tubing down through the ceiling hole. Attach the lower tubing ring to the ceiling frame ring and fasten it with screws. Attach the gasket to the diffuser lens and work the gasket around the perimeter of the ceiling frame. Repack any insulation around the tubing in the attic.

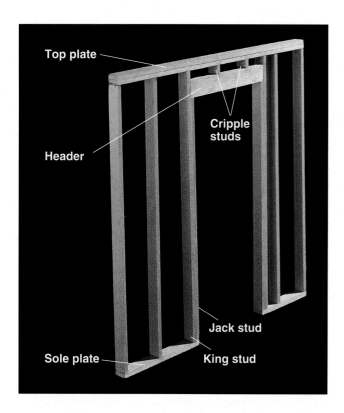

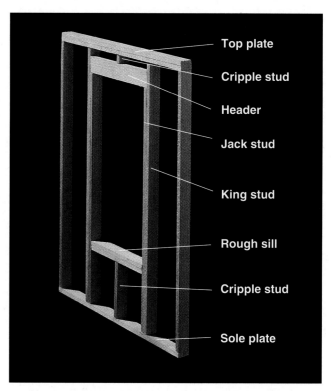

Framing for a New Door or Window

Installing a new door or window where one has never existed is a major project. But the transformation brought on by the new view, improved lighting, or more convenient access can be well worth the effort. Follow the general preparation and framing techniques shown here whether you are installing a standard exterior door, a glass patio door (page 108), or any standard window (page 111).

Adding a new door or window usually involves removing one or more studs in a load-bearing wall to make the opening. The new opening requires a permanent support beam, called a header, above the opening, to carry the structural load above. The required size for the header is set by local building codes and varies according to the width of the rough opening (chart, right).

If you will be removing more than one wall stud, make temporary supports to carry the structural load until the header is installed (page 103).

Everything You Need:

Tools: Stud finder, pencil, tape measure, chalk line, circular saw, utility knife, hammer, prybar, safety goggles, ratchet, hydraulic jacks, drill and spade bit, reciprocating saw, handsaw, nippers, 2-ft. level.

Materials: 2 × 4 lumber, 8d nails, 10d nails, ⅜ × 4" lag screws, ⅜" plywood, straight 1 × 4, shims.

NOTE: The following projects for framing and installing a new patio door or window (pages 102-115) show techniques for a platform-framed house with wood siding and wallboard interiors. To determine the type of framing used in your home, you may have to remove the wall surface at the bottom of the wall. Most houses built after 1930 use platform framing, which can be identified by the sole plates and top plates to which the studs are attached. If your house framing has long studs that run from the roof to the foundation sill plate, without the sole plates and top plates, contact a professional to do the framing.

Rough Opening Width	Recommended Header Construction
Up to 3 ft.	⅜" plywood between two 2 × 4s
3 ft. to 4 ft.	⅜" plywood between two 2 × 6s
4 ft. to 6 ft.	⅜" plywood between two 2 × 8s
6 ft. to 7 ft.	⅜" plywood between two 2 × 10s
7 ft. to 8 ft.	⅜" plywood between two 2 × 12s

Recommended header sizes are suitable for projects where a full story and roof are located above the rough opening. This chart is intended for rough estimates only. Always confirm your plans with your local building inspector.

How to Build Temporary Supports (Joists Parallel to the Wall)

1 Build a top plate 4 ft. longer than the wall opening from two 2 × 4s nailed together. Make two 4-ft.-long cross braces, using pairs of nailed 2 × 4s. Attach the cross braces to the top plate, 1 ft. from the ends, using countersunk lag screws.

2 Place a 2 × 4 sole plate directly over a floor joist, then set hydraulic jacks on the sole plate. For each jack, build a post 8" shorter than the jack-to-ceiling distance. Nail the posts to the top plate, 2 ft. from the ends. Cover the braces with the cloth, and set the support structure on the jacks.

3 Adjust the support structure so the posts are exactly plumb, and pump the hydraulic jacks until the cross braces just begin to lift the ceiling. Do not lift too far, or you may damage the ceiling or floor.

How to Build Temporary Supports (Joists Perpendicular to the Wall)

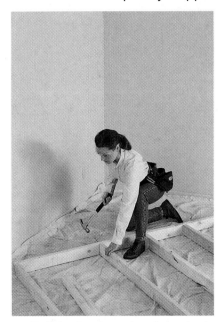

1 Build a 2 × 4 stud wall that is 4 ft. wider than the planned wall opening and 1¾" shorter than the distance from floor to ceiling.

2 Raise the stud wall up and position it 3 ft. from the wall, centered on the planned rough opening.

3 Slide a 2 × 4 top plate between the temporary wall and the ceiling. Check to make sure the wall is plumb, and drive shims under the top plate at 12" intervals until the wall is wedged tightly in place.

How to Remove Wallboard

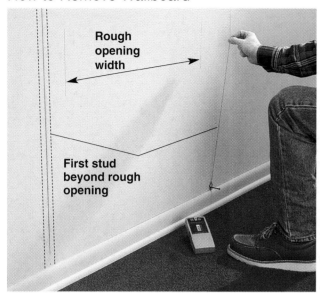

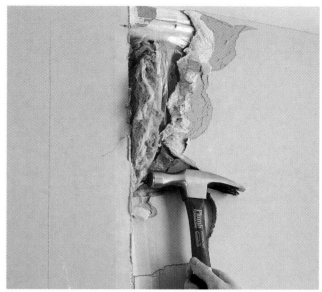

1 Shut off the power and check the installation area for hidden wiring or plumbing lines. Mark the width of the rough opening on the wall and locate the first stud on either side of the planned rough opening. Use a chalk line to mark the cutting lines down the centers of the wall studs. The exposed portion of each stud will provide a surface for attaching new wallboard when finishing the room.

2 Remove the wall trim. Set a circular saw to cut through the depth of the wallboard (usually ½"). Make a floor to ceiling cut along both lines. Finish the cuts at the top and bottom and along the horizontal seams with a utility knife. Starting at a cut corner, break away wallboard using a hammer claw. Remove the wallboard by striking the surface with the side of a hammer, and pulling the wallboard away from the wall. Take care to avoid damaging the wallboard outside the project area.

How to Frame a Door or Window

1 Prepare the project site and remove the interior wallboard. Measure and mark the rough opening width on the sole plate. Mark the locations of the jack studs and king studs on the sole plate. Where practical, use the existing studs as king studs.

2 Measure and cut the king studs, as needed, to fit between the sole plate and the top plate. Position the king studs and plumb with a level. Toenail them to the sole plate with 10d nails.

3 Measuring from the floor, mark the rough opening height on one of the king studs. The recommended rough opening for most doors or windows is ½" taller than the height of the door jamb or window frame. This line marks the bottom of the header.

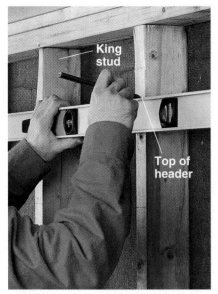

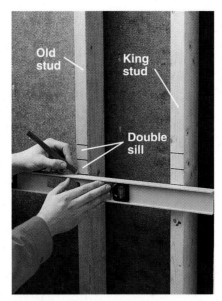

4 Measure and mark where the top of the header will fit against the king stud. The header size depends on the distance between the king studs (page 102). Use a level to extend the lines across the old studs to the opposite king stud. Make temporary supports if removing more than one stud (page 103).

Variation: For a window, measure down from the header line and outline the double rough sill on the king stud. Use a level to extend the lines across the old studs to the opposite king stud.

5 Set a circular saw to its maximum blade depth, then cut through the old studs along the lines marking the top of the header. For a window, also cut along the bottom of the rough sill. Do not cut the king studs.

6 Make an additional cut 3" below the top cut on each stud, using the circular saw. Then finish all the cuts with a handsaw.

7 Knock out the 3" stud sections, then tear out the rest of the studs with a pry bar. Clip away any exposed nails, using nippers.

8 Cut two jack studs to reach from the top of the sole plate to the bottom header lines on the king studs. Nail the jack studs to the king studs with 10d nails driven every 12".

(continued next page)

How to Frame a Door or Window (continued)

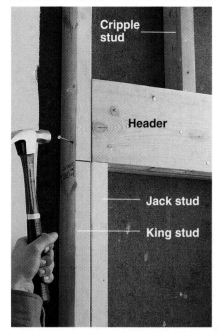

9 Build a header using two pieces of 2 × lumber sandwiched around ⅜" plywood (page 102). Position the header on the jack studs, using a hammer if necessary. Attach the header to the king studs, jack studs, and cripple studs, using 10d nails.

Variation: For a window, build the rough sill to reach between the jack studs by nailing a pair of 2 × 4s together. Position the rough sill on the cripple studs, and nail it to the jack studs and cripple studs with 10d nails.

Variation: For a door, use a reciprocating saw to cut through the sole plate next to each jack stud, then remove the sole plate with a pry bar. Cut off any exposed nails or anchors, using nippers.

How to Remove Exterior Wood Siding

1 From inside, drill through the wall at the corners of the framed opening. Push casing nails through the holes to mark their locations. For round-top windows, drill several holes around the curved outline.

2 Measure the distance between the nails on the outside of the wall to make sure the dimensions are accurate. Mark the cutting lines with a chalk line stretched between the nails. Push the nails back through the wall.

3 Tack a straight 1 × 4 to the wall so its edge is flush against the inside of one of the cutting lines. Drive the nails flush with the surface. Set the blade depth on a circular saw to cut through the siding and the sheathing, taking into account the thickness of the 1 × 4. NOTE: Use an old saw blade or a remodeling blade, as you're likely to hit nails as you cut through the siding.

4 Rest the saw on the 1 × 4, and cut along the chalk line, using the edge of the board as a guide. Stop the cut about 1" from each corner to avoid cutting into the framing. Reposition the board, and make the remaining cuts. Be sure to wear safety goggles while cutting through siding.

Variation: For round-top windows, make curved cuts, using a reciprocating saw or jig saw. Move the saw slowly to ensure smooth cuts.

6 Complete the cuts at the corners with a reciprocating saw or jig saw, being careful not to cut into the framing.

7 Remove the cut-out wall section. You may want to remove the siding pieces from the sheathing and save them for future use.

Installing a Patio Door

Blend your indoor and outdoor homes with a double glass patio door. For easy installation, buy a patio door with the panels already mounted in a preassembled frame. Try to avoid patio doors with frame kits that require complicated assembly.

Because patio doors have very long bottom sills and top jambs, they are susceptible to bowing and warping. To avoid these problems, be very careful to install the patio door so it is level and plumb, and to anchor the unit securely to framing members. Yearly caulking and touch-up painting helps prevent moisture from warping the jambs.

This project shows techniques for a house with wood siding. If you have vinyl or metal siding, consult your manufacturer for alternative installation methods.

Everything You Need:

Tools: Pencil, hammer, circular saw, chisel, stapler, caulk gun, pry bar, level, cordless screwdriver, handsaw, drill and bits, nail set.

Materials: Shims, drip edge, building paper, paintable silicone caulk, 10d casing nails, 8d nails, 3" wood screws, sill nosing, patio door kit, fiberglass insulation.

How to Install a Patio Door

1 Complete all prep work and framing required (see pages 102-107). Test-fit the door unit, centering it in the rough opening. Check to make sure door is plumb. If necessary, shim under the lower side jamb until the door is plumb and level. Have a helper hold the door in place while you adjust it.

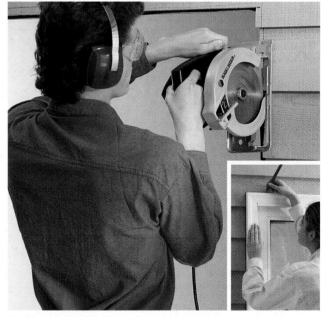

2 Trace the outline of the brick molding onto the siding, then remove the door unit (inset). Cut the siding along the outline, just down to the sheathing, using a circular saw. Stop short of the corners and finish the cuts with a sharp wood chisel.

Drip edge

3 To provide an added moisture barrier, cut a piece of drip edge to fit, then slide it between the siding and the existing building paper at the top of the opening. Cut 8"-wide strips of building paper and slide them between the siding and sheathing. Bend the paper around framing members and staple (inset).

4 Apply silicone caulk around the top and sides of the opening, where the siding meets the building paper (inset). Also apply several thick beads of caulk to the subfloor at the bottom of the door opening.

5 Center the patio door unit in the rough opening so the brick molding is tight against the sheathing. Make sure door threshold is level. If necessary, shim under the lower side jamb until the door is level.

6 If there are gaps between the threshold and subfloor, insert shims coated with caulk into the gaps, spaced every 6". Shims should be snug, but not cause bowing of the threshold. Clear off any excess caulk immediately.

7 Insert pairs of shims every 12" into the gap between the top jamb and the header and between the side jambs and the jack studs.

(continued next page)

8 From outside, drive 10d casing nails, spaced every 12", through the brick molding and into the framing members. Use a nail set to drive the nail heads below the surface of the wood.

9 From inside, drive 8d nails through the door jambs and each shim into the framing members. Set each nail head in with a nail set. Trim the shims flush with the framing and fill any gaps with loosely packed insulation.

10 Remove one of the screws found in the center of the threshold. Replace the screw with a 3" wood screw driven into the subfloor as an anchor.

11 Reinforce and seal the edge of the threshold by installing sill nosing under the threshold and against the wall. Drill pilot holes and attach the sill nosing with 10d casing nails. Apply paintable silicone caulk completely around the sill nosing, pressing caulk into any cracks.

12 Apply caulk around the top and sides of the brick molding where it meets the siding and in all exterior nail holes. Install the lockset as directed by the manufacturer. Paint over any nail holes and the sill nosing. See pages 114-115 for tips on finishing the interior walls and trim.

Installing a Window

Adding a new window instantly changes the entire atmosphere of a room by increasing ambient light and improving ventilation. Virtually every type of window—from a traditional double-hung to a large picture window—is suitable for do-it-yourself installation.

Many windows must be custom-ordered several weeks in advance. To save time, do the interior framing (pages 102-106) before the window arrives. However, don't remove the exterior wall surface (pages 106-107) until you have the window and are ready to install it.

Everything You Need:

Tools: 2-ft. level, hammer, reciprocating saw, circular saw, chisel, stapler, nail set, utility knife, caulk gun.

Materials: Window, 10d galvanized casing nails, 8d casing nails, shims, building paper, drip edge, fiberglass insulation, paintable silicone caulk.

How to Install a Window

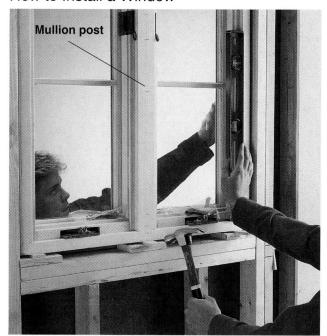

1 Set the window into the frame from the outside. Slide shims (and small wood blocks, if necessary) under the side jambs and mullion post so that the window is centered in the opening from side to side and top to bottom. Use the level to make sure the window is perfectly plumb and level, adjusting the shims as needed.

2 Trace the outline of the brick molding onto the siding. Remove the window, and cut the siding along the outline just down to the sheathing, using a reciprocating saw held at a low angle (inset). For straight cuts, you can use a circular saw.

(continued next page)

3 Cut 8"-wide strips of building paper and slide them behind the siding and around the entire window frame, then staple them in place. Cut a length of drip edge to fit over the top of the window, and fit its back flange between the siding and sheathing. Use flexible drip edge for round-top windows and rigid drip edge for straight-top units.

4 Reset the window and push the brick molding tight against the sheathing. Use the level to make sure the window is plumb and level, and adjust the shims, if necessary. Drive a 10d galvanized casing nail through the brick molding and into the frame at each corner.

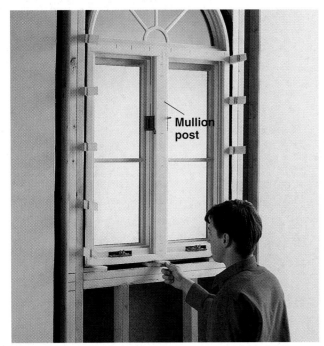

5 Adjust the shims so they are snug, but not so tight that they cause the jambs to bow. On multiple-unit windows, make sure the shims under the mullion posts are tight.

6 Use a straightedge to check the side jambs to make sure they do not bow. If necessary, adjust the shims until the jambs are flat. Open and close the window to make sure it works properly.

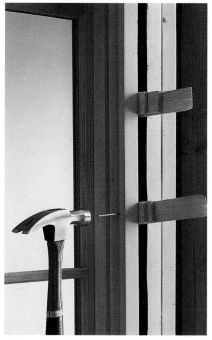
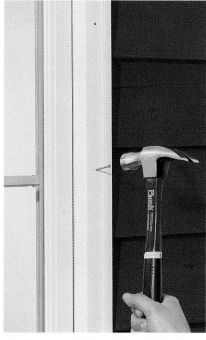

7 At each shim location, drill a pilot hole and drive an 8d casing nail through the jamb and into the frame. Set the nails with a nail set. Trim the shims flush to the frame, then fill the gaps behind the jambs with loosely packed insulation.

8 From outside, drive 10d galvanized casing nails, spaced every 12", through the brick moldings and into the framing members. Drive all nail heads below the wood surface with a nail set.

9 Apply paintable silicone caulk around the entire window unit. Fill all nail holes with caulk. See pages 114-115 for tips on finishing the interior walls and trim.

Variation: Masonry Clips

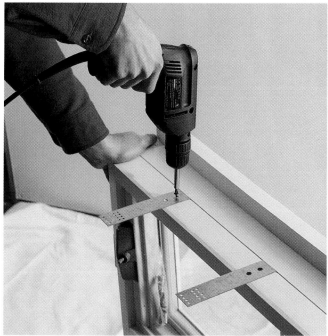

Metal masonry clips can be used if you want to avoid making nail holes in the surface of the brick molding. The masonry clips hook into precut grooves in the window jambs and are attached to the jambs with screws (left).

After setting the window in the frame, bend the masonry clips around the framing members and anchor them with screws (right).

Finishing a Door or Window Installation

Once your new door or window is installed, the final step is repairing and finishing the interior wall and adding any casing trim.

When installing wallboard around a door or window, cut L-shaped pieces that leave the joints centered over the door or window, not at the corners. Joints at corners often crack or bulge and can interfere with window and door trim.

Once the wallboard has been finished and sanded, the jamb and the wallboard should be sanded flush in order for the trim casings to fit properly. If they are not flush, use a block plane to shave down the protruding jamb, or use a surface-forming rasp to shave a protruding wallboard edge.

Stain the casings prior to installation or, if you plan to paint the casings, prime them before you install and paint after the nail holes have been filled with putty.

To ensure precise miter cuts that make tight joints, use a power miter saw, if you have one; otherwise, make cuts with a miter box and backsaw.

Everything You Need

Tools: Pencil, combination square, tape measure, level, straightedge, miter saw, hammer, nail set, sandpaper, utility knife, drill, wallboard knives, wallboard mud pan.

Materials: Wallboard, 1¼" wallboard screws, all-purpose wallboard joint compound and joint tape, casing material, 4d and 6d finish nails, wood putty.

How to Install Door & Window Casings

1 Mark a reveal line ⅛" from the inside edge of each jamb using a combination square. Place a length of casing flush with the reveal line and mark the points on the molding where horizontal and vertical reveal lines meet.

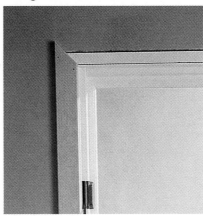

2 Make 45° miter cuts on the edge of each side casing. Drill pilot holes spaced every 12" and attach the vertical pieces to the jamb with 4d finish nails. Then drill pilot holes and drive 6d finish nails into the framing members near the outside edge of the casings.

3 Measure and cut the horizontal pieces to fit. Drill pilot holes and attach the casing with 4d and 6d finish nails. Locknail the corner joints by drilling pilot holes and driving 4d finish nails through each corner, as shown. Drive all nail heads below the wood surface, using a nail set, then fill the nail holes with wood putty.

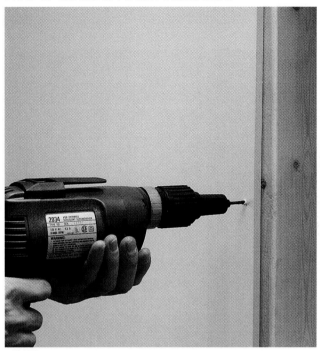

1 Install cut panels of wallboard over the unfinished area. Anchor the panels to the framing with 1¼" wallboard screws, spaced every 10". The screw heads should be sunk just below the surface, creating a slight depression in the paper without breaking through it.

2 Apply a thin layer of wallboard joint compound over the joints with a 4" or 6" wallboard knife. Load the knife by dipping it into a wallboard mud pan filled with joint compound.

3 Press the wallboard tape into the compound immediately, centering the tape over the joint. Smooth over the tape firmly with the 6" wallboard knife to flatten the tape and squeeze out excess compound from behind it. Let the compound dry completely.

4 Apply two thin finish coats of joint compound with a 10" or 12" wallboard knife. Allow the second coat to dry and shrink overnight before applying the final coat. Let the final coat dry completely before sanding. Cover all exposed screw heads with three coats of compound.

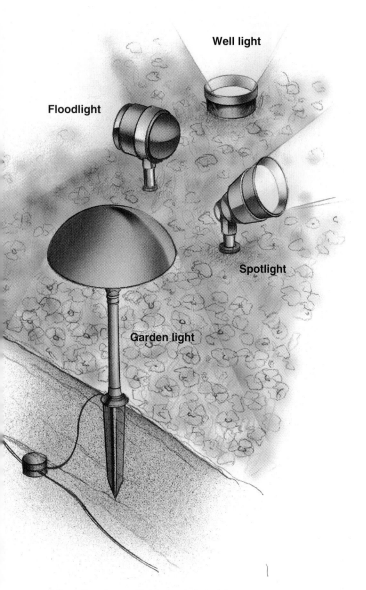

Well light

Floodlight

Spotlight

Garden light

Installing Landscape Lighting

A low-voltage lighting system will make your yard and landscape safer and more attractive. It's a good addition if you're also doing other improvements to the landscape.

When planning your lighting design, keep in mind that the most effective landscape lighting designs are created with a less-is-more philosophy. Overlighting, which is a common mistake, can make the landscape less inviting and disturb neighbors. Good lighting designs focus on the glow of the lights and the illuminated objects, not the bulbs or fixtures. To achieve this effect, selectively position lights in unobtrusive places, such as garden beds, the eaves of a pergola, behind shrubs, or even shining down from tree branches.

Always consider areas that need to be illuminated for safety or security reasons. Stairs, pathways, entrances, driveways, and garages often require additional light.

Everything You Need:

Tools: Screwdriver, trenching spade, ruler.

Materials: Low-voltage lighting kit, outdoor-grade PVC conduit, pipe straps with screws.

Tips for Landscape Lighting

"Shadow Lighting" casts the shadow of an interesting object onto a fence or wall that is directly behind the object.

"Uplighting" is achieved with floodlights or well lights, positioned to shine directly up at an object. Use uplighting to highlight trees, walls or outdoor sculpture.

"Sidelighting" uses a series of small, horizontally mounted spotlights to light a surface.

How to Install Low-voltage Landscape Lighting

1 Mount the control box on an outside wall, close to a GFCI receptacle. Dig a narrow trench for the light cable, about 6" to 8" deep, from the wall out about 1 ft. Measure from the control box to the bottom of the trench and cut a section of PVC conduit to this length. Feed the cable through the conduit, then position the conduit against the wall, with its bottom resting in the trench. Secure the conduit to the wall using pipe straps.

2 Starting at the end of the conduit, lay out the cable along the ground. Since you'll need to bury the cable, select a path with few obstacles. Assemble each fixture according to the manufacturer's directions.

3 Starting closest to the control box, plant each fixture by driving its stake firmly into the ground. Attach each fixture to the cable by tightening the cable connector cap, piercing the cable.

4 Turn on the lights and survey the system from several areas, making adjustments as needed.

5 Cut a narrow trench about 6" to 8" deep along the cable path, then gently install the cable and close the trench.

Installing a Floodlight

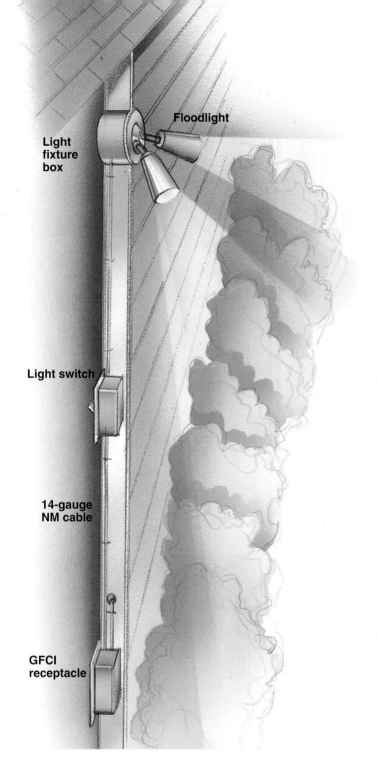

Floodlight

Light fixture box

Light switch

14-gauge NM cable

GFCI receptacle

Everything You Need:

Tools: Hammer, jig saw, cable ripper, wire combination tool, screwdriver.

Materials: Plastic light fixture box, plastic switch box, 14-gauge NM cable, cable staples, floodlight with hardware, wire connectors, single pole switch.

Floodlights provide illumination for outdoor spaces frequently used at night, such as barbecue areas, basketball courts, and garage entrances. Consider installing a light with a motion-sensor unit for added security and convenience. Motion sensors provide not only security, but energy savings, as well.

In this project, we'll show you how to mount a motion-sensor floodlight on your garage. The light and its switch are wired into an existing GFCI receptacle located inside the garage.

How to Install Floodlights

1 Turn off power to the GFCI receptacle to which you'll be wiring the light. Mark the position for the fixture box against the inside of the garage wall, adjacent to a stud. Drill a pilot hole, then cut the hole with a jig saw. Attach the box to the stud by hammering in the premounted nails.

2 Attach the switch box to a stud near the receptacle. Run one cable from the fixture to the switch and another from the switch to the receptacle, allowing an extra 1 ft. at each end. Anchor the cables to the framing with cable staples. Strip 10" of sheathing from the cable ends and ¾" of insulation from the wires.

3 Open a knockout in the fixture box and insert the cable. Assemble the light fixture according to manufacturer's instructions. Attach a bare copper wire to the grounding screw on the fixture. From outside, attach the wires on the light fixture to the corresponding circuit wires, using wire connectors.

4 Open knockouts on the top and bottom of the switch box and insert cables. Attach a copper pigtail to the grounding screw on the switch. Connect the two grounding wires to the pigtail with wire connectors. Connect the two black leads to the screw terminals on the switch. Connect the two white wires together with a wire connector. Tuck all the wires inside the box, secure the switch, and install the faceplate.

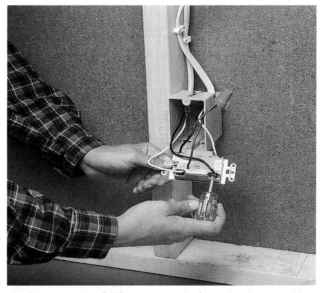

5 Remove the GFCI receptacle from the box and insert the cable into a knockout. Join the grounding pigtail on the GFCI to both circuit grounding wires. Attach the wires from the power source to the LINE terminals on the GFCI, the white wire to the silver terminal and black to brass. Attach the wires running from the switch to the LOAD terminals on the GFCI, white to silver and black to brass. Tuck the wires back into box, secure the receptacle and install the cover; restore the power.

Planting Trees

Trees help your landscape look more complete and add vertical interest to your yard. They also increase the value of the property. Planting trees in formation, similar to a hedge, creates a privacy screen, reduces noise, and protects your house from strong winds. You can also plant a single tree that will, at mature height, form a graceful ceiling for an area of your landscape.

Selecting Trees

Nurseries and garden centers sell trees packaged in three different ways. Each packaging method has advantages and disadvantages.

Container-grown trees are packed in pots of soil and are available in many sizes.

Bare-root trees are dug up during dormancy, so the branches and roots are bare. The roots are exposed and must be kept moist and protected from sun and wind damage during transport and before planting.

Balled-and-burlapped (B&B) trees are established trees with a large compact root ball that's tightly secured in burlap. Balled-and-burlapped trees are very heavy, and require special care when transporting. The soil and roots must not dry out before planting.

Transporting Trees

All trees need protection during transport. Because this can be a difficult process, many people opt to pay the nursery a delivery fee to handle the job. But, if you have access to a pickup or trailer, you can save money by transporting the tree yourself. Branches, foliage, and roots must be protected from breakage, and wind and sun damage, during transport. To protect your new tree, wrap it in burlap tied with twine. Secure the tree inside the truck bed with straps or rope. Drive slowly and carefully, especially around corners, and unload the tree by lifting it only by the roots, not the trunk.

How to Prepare the Planting Hole

The planting hole is one of the greatest contributing factors to the health of a tree. To prepare the hole, start by digging a hole two to three times as wide as the root ball of the B&B or container-grown tree. If you're planting a bare-root tree, the hole should be two to three times wider than the spread of the branches. To help the roots develop horizontally, slope the sides of the hole toward the surface. When finished, the hole should resemble a wide, shallow basin.

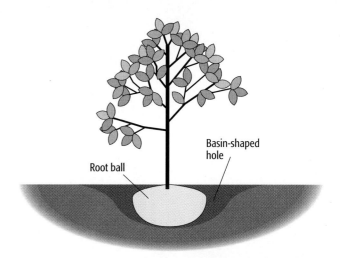

Root ball

Basin-shaped hole

How to Plant Bare-Root Trees

The roots of bare-root trees should be planted at a depth that is slightly higher than that at which they were originally grown. Start by slightly backfilling the planting hole with the soil you removed. Hold the tree in the hole; if the tops of the roots are still below the top of the hole, backfill more soil into the hole. Position the tree so that the largest branches are facing southwest, then spread out the roots. Backfill into the hole, covering the roots. As you backfill, gently lift the tree up and down to prevent air pockets from forming. When the hole is three-quarters full, tamp the soil and water it generously to remove any remaining air pockets. Completely fill the hole with soil, and lightly tamp it.

Position bare-root trees so that the largest branches face southwest. Then spread the roots out in the soil before backfilling the planting hole.

How to Plant B&B and Container-Grown Trees

Carefully set the B&B tree in the hole. Add or remove soil until the root ball rests slightly above ground level. Cut and remove the twine at the top of the ball. Cut the burlap away from top and sides of the rootball and remove as much of it as possible. For a container-grown tree, just remove the container before setting it in the hole. Backfill until the hole is three-quarters full. Lightly tamp the soil down, then water it slowly to remove any air pockets. Finish backfilling the hole, and tamp the soil.

(left) Cut and remove the twine from the top of balled-and-burlapped trees. Cut the burlap away, and remove it from around the tree.

(below) Trees are sold in several forms: bare root (A), container grown (B) and balled-and-burlapped (C).

Caring for New Trees

Trees require routine maintenance—especially during the first year. It takes almost a full year for a newly planted tree to establish a healthy root system. During the root development period, routine waterings are very important.

The best method for watering trees is to place a garden hose adjusted to release water in a slow trickle at the base of the tree for several hours. With this method, you can easily water the soil around the tree to a depth of 6" to 8". Use this method to water new trees any time the moisture depth in the soil is less than 6". In addition to watering, encourage root development by applying a fertilizer formulated for trees, every two to three years. Apply the fertilizer according to the directions on the label.

A

B

C

Preparing Soil for New Lawns

Renovating a lawn can have a truly dramatic effect on the look of your home, and soil preparation is the most important step in establishing a new lawn or other living ground cover. When you're starting from scratch, good soil preparation ensures that your lawn has the foundation it needs to develop a strong, healthy root system. Whether you're using sod, grass seed, or planting another ground cover, the process of preparing the soil remains the same.

Sizing up your Soil

The first step in soil preparation is finding out the condition of your existing soil. Start by getting a test done on the soil in the area where you plan to establish a lawn. For a small fee, a local soil testing lab or your state's agricultural extension service will conduct a detailed

To amend the soil, begin by spreading an even layer of the prescribed amendments over the area. Then use a tiller to blend the amendments into the soil, working in a small area at a time.

analysis of a soil sample from your yard. The soil test report will include information on the type of soil you have, the nutrient levels present and whether or not the soil is capable of supporting a healthy lawn. If the soil is within a desirable range, the report will also include detailed instructions for amending and fertilizing it.

Amending the Soil

If the test report indicates that you merely need to amend the soil, purchase the recommended amendments and rent a tiller to blend them into the soil.

Following manufacturer's instructions, set the tiller so that it digs to a depth between 4" and 6" (see photo, opposite page). Spread an even layer of the amendments over the surface of a small area and till them into the soil. Work your way across the yard in the same pattern you would use for mowing the grass. Once the entire lawn area is tilled, regrade and level the soil as necessary.

Bringing in New Soil

If your soil fails the lawn compatibility test, don't despair. You can purchase high-quality topsoil to add to your existing soil. Topsoil, also called "black dirt," is sold by the cubic yard and can be delivered by soil contractors (photo, below).

It's important not to create two distinct layers of soil, so you need to prepare the existing soil to mix with the new topsoil. Dig several small holes, then inspect and feel the texture of the existing soil. If it isn't se-

verely compacted, you can simply loosen it with a tiller before adding topsoil. If, on the other hand, the existing soil is heavily compacted, hire a contractor to "slice" it before you add the topsoil. Slicing is performed by heavy machinery outfitted with a blade. The blade makes deep cuts into the soil, loosening it up and eliminating compaction.

When you order topsoil, give the contractor the dimensions of your lawn and order enough topsoil to spread a 4" layer over the entire area. If you're covering a large area, you may want to hire the contractor to distribute the soil as well as deliver it.

Even if the area you're covering seems manageable, consider asking friends or hiring someone to help you spread the soil. It's not difficult, but it takes some time and effort. Drop wheelbarrow loads of soil around the area, then use a rake to distribute the soil evenly over the entire surface. When all the soil is distributed, check and correct the grade of the yard. When graded correctly, your yard should have a gradual slope away from the house of about ¾" per horizontal foot.

Smoothing the Surface

To create a smooth, even surface for seeding, sodding or planting ground cover, you'll need to slightly compress the soil. The goal is to lightly smooth the surface without compacting the soil. Fill a landscape drum ⅓ full with water, then roll it over the surface, walking in a row-by-row pattern (photo, below).

Order enough topsoil to spread a 4" to 6" layer over your existing soil. Before you spread new topsoil, loosen existing soil with a tiller or hire a contractor to "slice" the soil.

Lightly compact the soil with a landscape drum. Roll it over the lawn, walking in a row-by-row pattern.

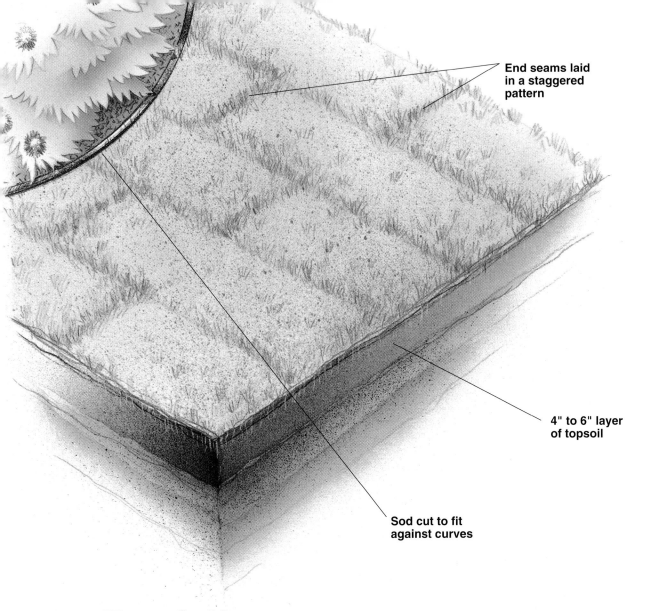

End seams laid in a staggered pattern

4" to 6" layer of topsoil

Sod cut to fit against curves

Installing a Sod Lawn

Installing sod is the quickest way to create a new lawn. Within a few hours, you can transform bare dirt into a lushly carpeted lawn. It's simple to create a beautiful lawn from sod, but it does require a little planning, thorough preparation, and some heavy work. To succeed, you need properly prepared soil, quality sod, careful installation, and adequate water.

Sod can be installed at any time from the beginning of the spring through early fall, but it's best to avoid installing it during especially hot, dry weather. You can purchase sod from a sod farm, landscape supply store or landscape contractor. When you compare prices, make sure all the quotes include delivery; most suppliers charge a fee for delivering small orders. For the best results, request that your sod be cut within 24 hours of delivery. After the sod arrives, store it in a shaded area, and install it within one day of delivery. Keep the sod moist, but don't soak it. Sod that dries out won't establish roots, but overwatered sod is heavy and difficult to install.

Good soil preparation is vital: the soil should be properly amended, smooth, and free from rocks or construction debris. Follow the guidelines on pages 124 to 125 to prepare the soil. Sod roots need to have contact with moist soil. If your soil is dry, water it the night before you plan to lay the sod.

Once the sod is laid, keep it constantly moist for three days. Following this period, water your lawn as often as needed to keep the first 4" of soil moist, making sure it receives around 1" to 1½" of water a week in rainfall and irrigation. During extended hot, dry weather, you'll need to water the sod frequently.

Everything You Need:

Tools: Sod knife, landscape drum, hose.

Materials: Fresh sod, topsoil, stakes.

How to Install Sod

1 Begin laying the sod against a straight border, such as a walkway, pressing the sod firmly into the soil. Then lay the next roll as close as possible to the first, butting the seams as closely as possible.

2 Lift up the edges of adjoining sod pieces, then press them down together, blending the seam between the pieces. As each new piece is laid, cover the seams with ½" of topsoil to prevent the edges from drying out.

3 Continue laying the sod, staggering the end seams. When sodding a slope, drive wooden stakes through the sod, 4" to 6" into the soil, to hold the sod in place. Use a sod knife to trim excess sod around walkway curves, planting beds, or trees.

4 After installing all of the sod, use a half-filled landscape drum to seat it firmly into the soil. Water the sod until it's thoroughly saturated.

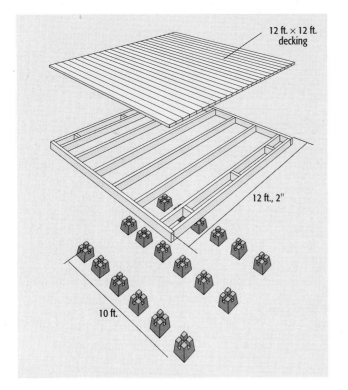

Building a Platform Deck

Perfect for entertaining or sunning yourself, this easy-to-build platform deck makes a great addition to your outdoor home. It can be built directly adjacent to your house, outside a set of double patio doors, or as a freestanding island deck anywhere in your yard.

You'll be able to build this deck over a single weekend. It uses lumber in standard lengths, so you don't need to do a lot of cutting. In addition, this deck uses precast concrete footings, rather than poured footings. These precast footings are available at home improvement centers and lumberyards.

A deck built from a weather-resistant material, such as cedar, redwood, cypress, or pressure-treated pine, will last for years. Although these woods are outdoor-grade, sealing the ends of each 2 × 6 with a high-quality sealer/protectant before you begin will maintain the durability of the wood. Galvanized hardware, which resists rust and corrosion, helps a deck remain strong and stable.

Our 12 × 12-ft. deck rests on a 10 × 10-ft. base formed by 18 concrete footings arranged in three rows of six footings each. Joists are secured in slots in the tops of the footings, simplifiying the building process. If you're building the deck on sloped or uneven ground, you'll need to use 4 × 4 posts that fit in the center of the footings to level the joists (see page 130 for additional information).

Although this platform deck rests close to the ground, you may want to add a hand rail around two or three sides of the deck, especially if the deck will be used by young children or an elderly person. See the variation on page 131 to add a railing.

Everything You Need

Tools: Level, shovel, drill with bits and drivers, circular saw or power miter box.

Materials: (18) Precast concrete footings, (38) 12-ft. 2 × 6s, 3" galvanized deck screws, wood sealer/protectant.

(For Railing Variation: (3) 12-ft. 2 × 6s, (13) 8 ft. 2 × 2s, 2½" galvanized deck screws).

12 ft. × 12 ft. decking

12 ft., 2"

10 ft.

How to Build a Platform Deck

1 Measure a 10 × 10-ft area and position a footing at each corner. Square the footings by measuring from corner to corner and adjusting the footings until the diagonals are equal. Set a 2 × 6 into the slots across the back row and check with a level. Add or remove soil beneath the footing to level it. Center a footing between these corner footings and recheck for level. Repeat this process for the footings on the front row.

2 Position the remaining 12 footings equally spaced to create three rows. Adjust soil as necessary to bring the interior footings level with the front and back rows. Center the 12-ft. joists across each row of footings and check the joists once again for level. Adjust footings as necessary.

3 Install the right and left side joists by lining up a 2 × 6 flush against the ends of the joists with the ends extending equally past the front and back joists. Attach the side joist by driving a pair of deck screws into each joist. Install the front and back rim joists by positioning a 2 × 6 flush between the ends of the side joists, forming a butt joint at each end. Drive pairs of deck screws through the faces of the side joists into the ends of the rim joists.

4 Measure and cut six 2 × 6 sleepers to fit between the front and back joists and the rim joists. Seal the cut ends with wood sealer/protectant and let dry completely. Position one sleeper in each row of footings between the first joist and the rim joist. Attach each sleeper by driving a pair of galvanized deck screws through each of the joists and into the sleeper.

(continued next page)

5 Once the framing is complete, measure the diagonals from corner to corner. Adjust the framing as necessary until both diagonal measurements are equal. Have a helper hold one side of the framework while you push against the other.

6 Lay a 2 × 6 over the surface of the deck, perpendicular to the joists and flush with the rim joists. Secure this board with deck screws. Install the remaining decking. Use a framing square to set a ⅛" space between the boards. You may need to rip-cut the last decking board.

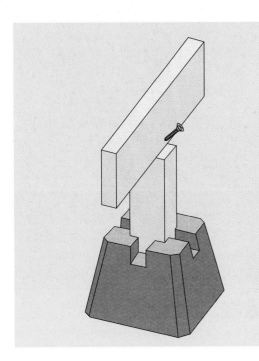

Tip: Leveling with Posts

If you're building your deck on sloped or uneven ground, you'll need to use 4 × 4 posts that fit in the center of the footings to level the joists.

Measure the distance between the bottom of the leveled joist and the square depression in the center of the footing. Measure, mark and cut a 4 × 4 post to this length. Place the post in the footing, then secure it by driving deck screws at an angle through the bottom of the joist into the post.

Variation: Adding a Railing

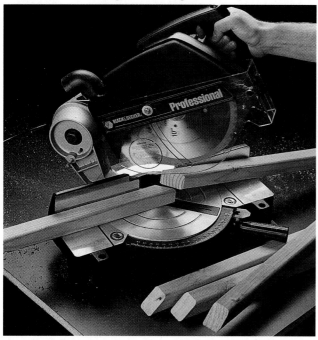

1 Cut 2 × 2s for the railing balusters at 42", using a power miter box or circular saw. Cut off the tops of the 2 × 2s square and cut the bottoms at a 45° angle. Seal the cut ends of lumber with wood sealer/protectant.

2 Place 2 × 2s flush together and adjust them so the ends are even. Draw a pair of straight lines, 3" apart, across each board, 1½" above the beveled end. Also draw lines 1½" and 4" from the other end. Using the lines as guides, drill ⅛" pilot holes into the 2 × 2s.

3 Position a 2 × 2 flush with the bottom of the joist, then clamp it into place to use as a placement guide. Position the corner 2 × 2s against the side joists, beveled end down, 4" in from the corner. Check for plumb, then drive deck screws through the pilot holes. Attach the remaining 2 × 2s for each side, spacing them 4" apart.

4 Attach a 12-ft. 2 × 6 behind the 2 × 2s, to form the top railing, using deck screws driven through the pilot holes. Connect the top rails in the corners, using pairs of deck screws.

Pouring a Concrete Walkway

Replacing a crackled, buckled sidewalk gives your yard a facelift, while installing an all-new length of walkway can improve its function. Walkways serve as the "hallways" between entryways to your home and heavily used areas of your yard.

This project introduces you to basic techniques for planning and laying out a concrete project as well as pouring and working with concrete. Mastering this project can prepare you for other, more complicated projects, such as laying a patio or a driveway. Remember, any concrete project will go more smoothly if you plan carefully, reserve an adequate amount of time, and recruit help.

Everything You Need:

Tools: Line level, hammer, shovel, sod cutter, wheelbarrow, tamper, drill, level, screed board, straightedge, mason's string, mason's float, mason's trowel, edger, groover, stiff-bristle broom.

Materials: Garden stakes, rebar, bolsters, 2 × 4 lumber, 2½" and 3" screws, concrete mix, concrete sealer, isolation board, compactible gravel, construction adhesive, nails.

Tips for Laying Out the Site

To make sure your layout is square, use the 3-4-5 triangle method: Measuring from a corner, mark a point 3 ft. out along one string and 4 ft. out along the intersecting string. Measure between the points, and adjust the string position until the distance between the points is exactly 5 ft.

Most concrete surfaces should have a slight slope away from the house to direct water runoff. To create a standard slope of ⅛" per foot, multiply the distance between stakes on one side (in feet) by ⅛. For example, if the stakes are 10 ft. apart, the result is ¹⁰⁄₈ (1¼"), and you'll move the strings down 1¼" on the stake on the low ends.

Tips for Estimating Concrete

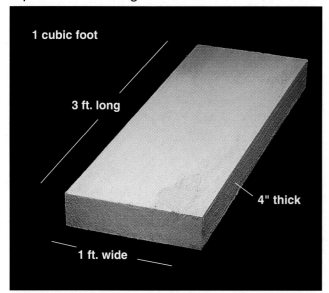

1 cubic foot

3 ft. long

4" thick

1 ft. wide

Measure the width and length of the project in feet, then multiply the dimensions to get the square footage. Measure the thickness in feet (4" thick equals ⅓ ft.), then multiply the square footage times the thickness to get the cubic footage. For example, 1 ft. × 3 ft. × ⅓ ft. = 1 cu. ft. A 60-lb. bag of premixed concrete yields roughly ½ cu. ft. Twenty-seven cubic feet equals one cubic yard, which can cover roughly 80 sq. ft. at a 4" thickness.

Understanding Bleed Water

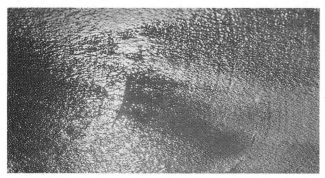

Timing is key to an attractive concrete finish. When concrete is poured, the heavy materials gradually sink, leaving a thin layer of water—known as *bleed water*—on the surface. To achieve an attractive finish, it's important to let bleed water dry before proceeding with other steps. Follow these rules to avoid problems:
- Settle and screed the concrete and add control joints immediately after pouring and before bleed water appears. Otherwise, surface cracks and other flaws are likely to appear.
- Let bleed water dry before floating or edging. Concrete should be hard enough that foot pressure leaves no more than a ¼"-deep impression.

NOTE: Bleed water does not appear with air-entrained concrete, which is used in regions where temperatures often fall below freezing.

Tips for Mixing Concrete

For larger jobs, such as walkways, it pays to rent a power mixer from a local concrete supplier or rental center. Depending upon the size, most power mixers are designed to mix either 3 or 9 bags at a time. For jobs larger than 1 cubic yard, have ready-mix concrete delivered to your site. Although it is more expensive, this method saves time.

Making a Curved Screed Board

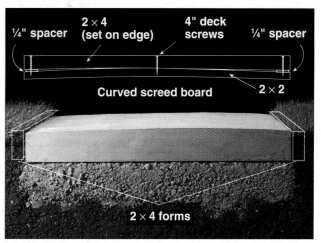

¼" spacer   2 × 4 (set on edge)   4" deck screws   ¼" spacer

Curved screed board   2 × 2

2 × 4 forms

Crown the walkway so it is ¼" higher at the center than at the edges. This will prevent water from pooling on the surface. To make the crown, construct a curved screed board by cutting a 2 × 2 and 2 × 4 long enough to rest on the walkway forms. Butt them together edge to edge and insert a ¼" spacer between them at each edge. Attach the parts with 4" deck screws driven at the center and the edges. The 2 × 2 will be drawn up at the center, creating a curved edge. Screed the concrete with the curved edge of the screed board facing down.

How to Build a Concrete Walkway

1 Select a rough layout, including any turns. Stake out the location and connect the stakes with mason's strings. Set the slope, if needed (see page 132). Remove sod between the lines and 6" beyond them, then excavate the site with a spade to a depth 4" greater than the thickness of the concrete walkway. Follow the slope lines to maintain consistent depth.

2 Pour a 5" layer of compactible gravel as a subbase for the walkway. Tamp the subbase until it compacts to an even 4"-thick layer.

3 Build and install 2 × 4 forms set on edge. Miter-cut the ends at angled joints. Position them so the inside edges are lined up with the strings. Attach the forms with 3" deck screws, then drive 2 × 4 stakes next to the forms at 3-ft. intervals. Attach the stakes to the forms with 2½" deck screws. Use a level to make sure forms are level or set to achieve the desired slope. Drive stakes at each side of angled joints.

4 Glue an asphalt-impregnated isolation board to the steps, house foundation, or other permanent structures that adjoin the walkway, using construction adhesive.

Variation: Reinforce the walkway with #3 steel rebar. For a 3-ft.-wide walkway, lay two sections of rebar spaced evenly inside the project area. Use bolsters to support the rebar (make sure rebar is at least 2" below the tops of the forms). Bend rebar to follow any angles or curves, and overlap pieces at angled joints by 12". Mark locations for control joints (to be cut with a groover later) by tacking nails to the outside faces of the forms, spaced roughly at 3-ft. intervals.

5 Mix, then pour concrete into the project area. Use a masonry hoe to spread it evenly within the forms. After pouring all of the concrete, run a spade along the inside edges of the form, then rap the outside edges of the forms with a hammer to help settle the concrete.

6 Build a curved screed board (see page 133) and use it to form a crown when you smooth out the concrete. NOTE: A helper makes this easier.

(continued next page)

How to Build a Concrete Walkway (continued)

7 Smooth the surface with a float. Cut control joints at marked locations using a trowel and a straight-edge. Let the concrete dry until any bleed water disappears (see page 133).

8 Shape the edges of the concrete by running an edger along the forms. Smooth out any marks created by the edger, using a float. Lift the leading edges of the edger and float slightly as you work.

9 Once any bleed water has disappeared, draw a groover along the control joints, using a straight 2 × 4 as a guide. Use a float to smooth out any tool marks.

10 Create a textured, non-skid surface by drawing a clean, stiff-bristled broom across the surface. Avoid overlapping broom marks. Cover the walkway with plastic and let the concrete cure for one week.

11 Remove the forms, then backfill the space at the sides of the walkway with dirt or sod. Seal the concrete, if desired, according to the manufacturer's directions.

Installing Brick Pavers Over Concrete

Give old concrete around your home a facelift with the warm, traditional look of brick pavers. The pavers are set into mortar directly over the existing concrete, eliminating the need to remove the old surface. Techniques shown here can be used to create projects like this step landing (left) that gives any home a more formal appearance. Or, transform a boring concrete slab into a charming brick patterned patio.

Before installing pavers, make sure the concrete is structurally sound and free of major cracks. If you are installing pavers next to your home, glue a ½" asphalt-impregnated isolation board to the house so the structures can move independently.

Everything You Need:

Tools: Brickset chisel and maul or brick splitter, shovel, level, rubber mallet, mortar bag, jointing tool, mason's trowel.

Materials: Brick pavers, isolation board (if necessary), type S mortar, 2 × 4, plastic sheeting.

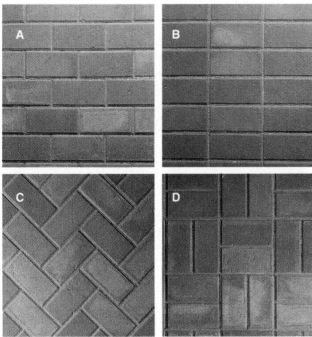

Standard bricks and pavers can be arranged in several patterns, including: Running bond (A), jack-on-jack (B), herringbone (C), or basket weave pattern (D). Jack-on-jack and basket weave require fewer cut pavers along the edges. Standard pavers have spacing lugs on the sides that automatically set the joints at ⅛" width.

To cut brick pavers, first score all four sides of the brick with a brickset chisel and maul. Tap the chisel to leave scored cutting marks ⅛" to ¼" deep, then strike a firm final blow to the chisel to split the brick. Properly scored bricks split cleanly with one firm blow. If your project requires many cuts, it is a good idea to rent a brick splitter, which makes accurate, consistant cuts with no scoring required (inset).

How to Install Brick Pavers over Concrete

1 Select a paver pattern (see page137). Dig a trench around the concrete, slightly wider than the thickness of one paver. Dig the trench so it is about 3½" below the concrete surface. Soak the pavers with water (dry pavers absorb moisture, weakening the mortar strength).

2 Sweep the old concrete, then hose off the surface and sides with water to clear away dirt and debris. Mix a small batch of mortar according to manufacturer's directions. For convenience, place the mortar on a scrap of plywood.

3 Install edging bricks by applying a 1½" layer of mortar to the side of the concrete slab and to one side of each brick. Set bricks into the trench, against the concrete. Brick edging should be 1½" higher than the thickness of the brick pavers.

4 Finish the joints on the edging bricks with a jointer (step 9), then mix and apply a ½"-thick bed of mortar to one end of the sidewalk, using a trowel. Mortar hardens very quickly, so work in sections no larger than 4 sq. ft.

5 Make a "screed" for smoothing mortar by notching the ends of a short 2 × 4 to fit between the edging bricks. Depth of the notches should equal the thickness of the pavers. Drag the screed across the mortar bed until the mortar is smooth.

6 Lay the paving bricks one at a time into the mortar, maintaining a ½" gap between pavers. (A piece of scrap plywood works well as a spacing guide.) Set the pavers by tapping them lightly with a rubber mallet.

7 As each section of pavers is completed, check with a level to make sure the tops of the pavers are even.

8 When all the pavers are installed, use a mortar bag to fill the joints between the pavers with fresh mortar. Work in 4-sq.-ft. sections, and avoid getting mortar on the tops of the pavers.

9 Use a jointer to finish the joints as you complete each 4-sq.-ft. section. For best results, finish the longer joints first, then the shorter joints. Use a trowel to remove excess mortar.

10 Let the mortar dry for a few hours, then remove any residue by scrubbing the pavers with a coarse rag and water. Cover the walkway with plastic and let the mortar cure for at least two days. Remove plastic, but do not walk on pavers for at least one week.

INDEX

A

Accessibility, 6-9
Air-entrained Concrete, 133
Appliances, Typical Wattage Ratings, 50
Attic, Running Electrical Cable into, 54
Audio System, see: Entertainment System

B

Baseboard Trim, 20-23
Basement, Running Electrical Cable into, 54
Basket Weave Pattern for Bricks, 137
Bathroom Design and Accessibility, 6, 7
Bleed Water in Concrete, 133
Blended Paint Finish, 12, 13
Booking Wallcovering, 16
Brick Molding, 111, 112
Brick Pavers,
    Cutting, 137
    Installing over concrete, 137-139
    Patterns, 137
Built-in Shelving, Constructing, 72, 73

C

Cabinets,
    Adding glide-out shelving, 74, 75
    Frameless, 84
    Installing new cabinets, 80-87
    Installing undercabinet lighting, 40, 41
    Universal design, 8
Cable, Electrical,
    Attaching connectors to, 59
    How to run, 54, 59
    Stripping NM cable, 51
Ceiling Fan-light, 44, 45
    Typical wattage rating, 50
Ceilings, 6
    Ceiling tile, 29-31
    Crown molding around, 20, 23-25
    Installing ceiling fan-light, 44, 45
    Installing crown molding lighting, 42, 43
    Installing custom light boxes, 46-48
    Installing incandescent fixtures, 38

    Installing tubular skylight, 100, 101
    Wallcovering on ceiling, 19
Cement Block Wall, Cutting Opening in, 66, 67
Ceramic Tile Backsplash, 32-35
    Cutting tile, 33
Circuit Capacity, Evaluating, 50
Closed-circuit Camera, 55
Closets, 6, 8
    See also: Storage & Shelving
Color Wash Paint Finish, 12, 15
Compound Miter Saw, 22
Computer,
    Networking, 55-60
    Typical wattage rating, 50
Concrete,
    Air-entrained concrete, 133
    Estimating concrete volume, 133
    Footings for deck, 128, 129
    Installing brick pavers over, 137-139
    Pouring concrete walkway, 132-136
    Understanding bleed water, 133
Coped Joint, 21, 22
Corners,
    Crown molding around, 24, 25
    Installing cabinets, 83, 86
    Miter joint, 21, 22, 25
    Wainscoting around, 26-28
    Wallcovering around, 18
Cripple Stud (shown on illustration), 102
Crown Molding, 20, 23-25
    Installing lighting along, 42, 43
Cutting Techniques,
    Brick, 137
    Cement block wall, 66, 67
    Ceramic tile, 33
    Trim molding, 22

D

Deadbolt Locks, 90, 91
    Replacing with keyless entry system, 93, 94
Deck, Building, 128-131
Dishwasher, Typical Wattage Rating, 50
Distribution Center for Home Network, 56, 58
Doors & Doorways,
    Door reinforcer, 90, 91
    Framing for new door, 102-107
    Installing casings, 114
    Installing garage door opener, 95-97
    Installing patio door, 108-110
    Installing storm door, 98, 99
    Keyless entry system, 9, 93, 94
    Security & locks, 90, 91, 93, 94
    Universal design, 6, 8, 9
    Wallcovering around, 19
Drip Edge, 109, 112

E

Electrical,
    Adding receptacle, 49-54
    Attaching connectors to cables, 59
    Common wattage ratings, 50
    Evaluating circuit capacity, 50
    How to connect wires, 51
    How to run cable, 54, 59
    How to strip cables & wires, 51
    Networking home, 55-60
    Pigtailing wires, 51
    Testing for power, 52
    See also: Lighting
Entertainment System,
    Networking, 55-60
    Typical wattage ratings, 50
Entry Doors, 90
    See also: Doors & Doorways
Entry Ramp for Wheelchair, 9
Exterior Siding, Removing, 106-108

F

Fan-light, Ceiling,
    Hanging, 44, 45
    Typical wattage rating, 50
F-connector Fittings & Terminals, 55, 59, 60
Fireplace, Gas, Installing, 63-69
Floodlight, Installing, 120, 121
Footings, Concrete, 128, 129
Forms for Concrete, Building, 134, 135
Foundation Wall, Cutting Opening in, 66, 67
Frameless Cabinets, 84
Framing,
    Determining framing style of house, 102
    For gas fireplace, 64, 65
    For new door or window, 102-107
    Identification of stud types, 102

G

Garage Door,
    Installing garage door opener, 95-97
    Security tips, 90
Garbage Disposal, Typical Wattage Rating, 50
Gardening,
    Installing new lawns, 124-127
    Planting trees, 122, 123
    Raised beds, 9
    Soil test, 124
Gas Fireplace, Installing, 63-69
Gas Leak, Checking for, 67
Glide-out Shelving, Building, 74, 75
Grab Bars, 6
Grass, see: Lawns
Grout, 35, 69

H

Handles, 8, 9
Hand Railing for Deck, 131
Header,
    Adding in load-bearing wall, 102, 106
    Recommended construction, 102
    Shown on illustration, 65, 102
Herringbone Pattern for Bricks, 137
Hinges, Increasing Security, 90, 91
Home Network System, 55-60

I

Icemaker, Connecting, 62
Internet Access, 55, 57

J

Jack-on-jack Pattern for Bricks, 137
Jack Stud (shown on illustration), 102
Joints for Molding, 21
Jury Stick, 33

K

Keyless Entry System, 9
    Installing, 93, 94
King Stud (shown on illustration), 102
Kitchen,
    Installing new cabinets, 80-87
    Installing water filtration system, 61, 62
    Tiling backsplash, 32-35

L

Landscaping,
    Building platform deck, 128-131
    Installing new lawns, 124-127
    Lighting, 9, 118, 119
    Planting trees 122, 123
    Pouring concrete walkway, 132-134
    Raised beds, 9
    Slope for runoff, 132
    Soil test, 124
    Universal design, 9
Latch Guard, 91
Lawns,
    Installing sod, 126, 127
    Soil preparation, 124, 125
Ledger Board, 82
Lighting,
    Ceiling fan-light, 44, 45
    Crown molding lighting, 42, 43
    Custom light boxes, 46-48
    Floodlight, 120, 121
    Incandescent fixtures, 38

    Landscape lighting, 9, 118, 119
    Rope lighting, 42, 43
    Switch locations, 7
    Switch styles, 7
    Track lighting, 39
    Undercabinet lighting, 40, 41
    Universal design, 7
Load-bearing Wall,
    Building temporary supports, 103
    Framing for new door or window, 102, 104-107
Locks,
    For doors & windows, 90-94
    Keyless entry system, 9, 93, 94
Low-voltage Landscape Lighting, 9, 118, 119

M

Masonry Clips, 113
Miter Box, 22
Mitered Joint, 21, 22, 25
Mobility Limitations, Designing for, 6-9
Molding, see: Trim Moldings
Mortar, Working with, 139
Motion-sensor Lighting, 120, 121
Mullion Post, 111
Multimedia, see: Entertainment System

N

Networking Home Systems, 55-60
NM Cable,
    How to run cable, 54, 59
    Stripping, 51
Noise Reduction, 6, 29

O

Outside Corner Miter, 21

P

Paints & Painting,
    Applying decorative finishes, 12-15
    Ceiling tile, 29
    Finish options, 6
    Patina effect, 29
    Universal design, 6
Patio Door,
    Installing, 108-110
    Security of sliding door, 90-92
Pattern for Stencilling, 15
Pavers, see: Brick Pavers
Phone, see: Telecommunications System
Physical Limitations, Designing for, 6-9
Pigtailing Electrical Wires, 51
Platform Deck, Building, 128-131

Platform-framed House, 102
Plumbing,
    Checking for gas leaks, 67
    Installing water filtration system, 61, 62
Polymer Crown Molding, 24, 25
    Installing lighting along, 42, 43

R

Railing for Deck, 131
Raised-bed Garden, 9
Receptacles,
    Adding, 49-54
    Connecting wires to, 51
    Location, 7, 49
Refrigerator,
    Icemaker, 62
    Typical wattage rating, 50
RJ45 Jacks, 55, 59, 60
Roller for Two-tone Painting, 13
Roof, Cutting Hole in for Skylight, 101
Rope Lighting, 42, 43
Running Bond Pattern for Bricks, 137
Runoff, 132

S

Scarf Joint, 21
Screed Board, 133
Security,
    Installing keyless entry system, 93, 94
    Networking home security system, 55-60
    Securing doors & windows, 90-94
Shelving, see: Storage & Shelving
Siding, Removing, 106-108
Sink, Installing Water Filtration System, 61
Skylight, Installing Tubular, 100, 101
Sliding Glass Doors,
    Installing patio door, 108-110
    Security, 90-92
Sliding Windows, Security, 92
Slope for Runoff, 132
Sodding a Lawn, 126, 127
    Soil preparation, 124, 125
Soil Preparation,
    For new lawns, 124, 125
    For planting trees, 122, 123
    Topsoil depth, 125
Sole Plate (shown on illustration), 102
Sponge for Color Washing, 14
Square,
    Determining in deck construction, 130
    3-4-5 triangle method, 132
Stairs & Stairwells,
    And universal design, 6
Stencilling, 12, 15
Stippling, 15

Storage & Shelving,
  Building glide-out shelving, 74, 75
  Building recessed shelving, 76-79
  Constructing built-in shelving, 72, 73
  Universal design, 6, 8
Storm Door, Installing, 98, 99
Stripping Electrical Cable, 51
Studs used in Framing, (Shown on
  Illustration), 102
Supports for Load-bearing Wall
  Removal, 103

T

Taping Wallboard, 115
Telecommunications System,
  Networking, 55-60
3-4-5 Triangle Method for Checking
  Square, 132
Tile,
  Around gas fireplace, 69
  Ceiling tile, 29-31
  Ceramic tile backsplash, 32-35
Tongue-and-groove,
  Ceiling tile, 29-31
  Wainscoting, 26-28
Top Plate (shown on illustration), 102
Topsoil Depth, 125
Track Lighting, Installing, 39
Trees, Planting, 122, 123
Trim Moldings, 20-25
  Baseboard trim, 20-23
  Cap rail molding, 28
  Casings around doors & windows,
  114
  Crown molding, 20, 23-25

For cabinets, 85, 87
Tubular Skylight, Installing, 100, 101

U

Undercabinet Lighting, Installing,
  40, 41
Undersink Water Filtration System,
  Installing, 61
Universal Design, 6-9

V

Ventilation for Fireplace, 66, 67
Video System, see: Entertainment
  System
Visual Limitations, Designing for, 6-9

W

Wainscoting, 6
  Applying, 26-28
Walkways, 9
  Installing brick pavers over
  concrete, 137-139
  Pouring concrete walkway, 132-136
Wallboard,
  Finishing, 115
  Removing, 104
Wallpaper, 6
  Applying, 16-19
  Preparing wallpaper, 16
Walls & Wall Treatments,

Baseboard trim, 20-23
Building recessed shelving, 76-79
Crown molding, 20, 23-25
Installing wall cabinets, 80-85
Load-bearing wall, framing for new
  door or window, 102-107
Paint, 6, 12-15
Preparing walls for new cabinets, 81
Universal design, 6
Wainscoting, 6, 26-28
Wallcovering, 6, 16-19
Water Filtration System, 61, 62
Water Supply,
  Whole-house water filtration
  system, 62
Wattage Ratings of Common
  Appliances, 50
Wheelchair Accessibility, 6-9
  Entry ramp, 9
Windows,
  Framing for new window, 102-107
  Installing casings, 114
  Installing new window, 111-115
  Locations, 9
  Security & locks, 90, 92
  Universal design, 9
  Wainscoting around, 28
  Wallcovering around, 19
Wood Species,
  For platform deck, 128
  For trim moldings, 20

Contributors

Photographers

Karen Melvin
Architectural Stock Images, Inc.
Minneapolis, MN
©Karen Melvin: p. 7, and for the fol-
lowing designers: The Two of Us
Interior Design: pp. 10-11, 12 (cen-
ter); David Wenzel: p. 12 (bottom);
Woodshop of Avon: 32 (top)

Photo Contributors

Armstrong Ceilings
800-426-4261
www.armstrongceilings.com

The Balmer Studios, Inc.
1-800-665-3454
www.balmerstudios.com

Heatilator, Inc.
800-259-1549
www.heatilator.com

Kraftmaid Cabinetry, Inc.
800-571-1990
www.kraftmaid.com

Kwikset Corporation
714-535-8111
www.kwikset.com

Laufen Ceramic Tile
800-331-3651
www.laufenusa.com

National Closet Group
866-NCG-LINE
www.nationalclosetgroup.com

Pass &Seymour/legrand
800-223-4185
www.passandseymour.com

Pella Storm Doors
888-646-5354
www.pella.com

Sun Tunnel Skylights, Cambell, CA
800-369-7465
www.suntunnel.com

Wagner Spray Tech
763-553-7000
www.wagnerspraytech.com